Paths into
the Book *of*
Books

Paths into *the* Book *of* Books

New Biblical Translations through the Festivals of the Year

Elsbeth Weymann

Floris Books

Translated by Luke Barr

First published in German under the title *Wege im Buch der Bücher* in 2011 by Verlag Urachhaus, Stuttgart

First published in English in 2015 by Floris Books

© 2011 Verlag Freies Geistesleben & Urachhaus GmbH, Stuttgart
English version © 2015 Floris Books

All rights reserved. No part of this book may be reproduced in any form without permission of Floris Books, 15 Harrison Gardens, Edinburgh
www.florisbooks.co.uk

British Library CIP Data available
ISBN 978-178250-162-6
Printed in Poland

Contents

Introduction	11
Advent	**25**
Human soul, lift up your heart (Isaiah 60)	25
Expanse prepares my soul (Luke 1)	29
Christmas	**36**
Magi came from the rising sun (Matthew 2)	36
And shepherds were in this land (Luke 2)	41
Between Epiphany and Passiontide	**51**
I, I am he who speaks with you (John 4)	
Passiontide	**63**
Did not the Christ have to suffer these things? (Matthew 27 & Psalm 22)	
Easter Sunday	**75**
Mary of Magdala and the twice-turning (John 20)	
Eastertime	**85**
Were not our hearts burning within us? (Luke 24)	
Ascension	**95**
Why do you stand looking into the heavens? (Acts 1)	
Whitsun	**103**
Tongues, divided, as of fire (Acts 2)	
St John's Tide	**113**
He must increase, I must decrease (Mark 1)	

Michaelmas 124
The armour of God (Ephesians 6)

Advent 137
In the beginning – the Logos (John 1)

Notes 149

Bibliography 151

To students of my Greek lessons,
without whom this book
would not have been written

Read no more – look!
Look no more – go!
Paul Celan, 'Straitening' *(Engführung)*

Introduction

Translating is impossible, but very useful.
Swetlana Geier

This work has arisen out of many years teaching in the priest seminaries of The Christian Community in Stuttgart and Hamburg. The task there was to help lead the students so far into the Greek language, that through a recognition of certain grammatical forms, and through contemplating the range of meanings of particular words, other deeper levels of the texts would be revealed.

Origen (AD 185–253/54) describes three levels of meaning, a method to open up a text which was much used in the ancient world and in medieval times.[1] In this method, three levels of the text are differentiated:

1. The *literal or historical sense* establishes what is to be discovered in historical context or factual terms.
2. An understanding of the content of the text, and a recognised overall picture should emerge from the *moral sense.* The reader's personal impressions and sense of the text could be included here.
3. With the *spiritual or rising sense,* we leave the realm of the historical, literal, or even personal, and attempt to tease out the spiritual content.

A contemporary form of this appears to me to be found in Paul Celan's poem 'Straitening' *(Engführung).* The poem, which serves as the motto of this book, includes this trichotomy of meaning, when it says:

Read no more – look!
Look no more – go!

The first reference is to reading, which is simply the literal or historical sense. However, it demands to go further than that.

The second imperative, 'look' concerns a process of deepening reflection in order to perceive the overall coherence of the text with which the soul now begins to connect itself. This corresponds to Origen's moral sense.

The third level (the rising or spiritual sense) can also be traced in Celan's poem, 'Look no more – go!' With the rising sense, we are led upwards and our spiritual sense is awakened. This, however, is only possible if we have been inwardly active on all three levels – in reading, looking, and rising or *going*.

This work follows four guiding lights or points of reference on the 'paths into the Book of Books'.

1. To demonstrate, through concrete examples, how the living presence of the Old Testament is reflected in the New Testament.
2. To show and clarify what the grammatical form in a sentence construction or in the meaning of a word expresses.
3. To explain some of the text extracts using Origen's three levels of meaning.
4. To attempt a style perhaps more suited to a modern poem rather than using a prose style in the translations. Since all Bible texts were originally *spoken* texts, I would like to stay true to this form and offer texts which are suited to the rhythm of the breath. It is nonetheless important not to impose too contemporary a style, thereby losing the essence of the original. I have therefore consciously retained the seemingly 'unnecessary' tautology of these texts, and the quite frequent use of the repetitive form, such as 'and ... and ... and'.

Translation work

Anyone who has attempted translating, knows how difficult it is – metaphorically speaking – to 'cross over' from the shore of one language to the other. A completely congruent translation is impossible – each one is provisional and reveals the limitations of the translator. Nonetheless, a translation can act as a bridge, taking us into new land and opening up vistas in which spiritual knowledge can be viewed in a new context.

For instance, in the story of the raising of Lazarus in the Gospel of John, the decisive verse (11:43) is almost always translated as 'Lazarus, come forth!' However, when one reads the original text in Greek, a different connotation is discernible. The words used: Λαζαρε, δευρο ἐξω *(Lazare, deuro exo)* contain the name in the grammatical form of the vocative (being called on, or addressed) whereby a quite personal invocation is spoken. What is missing in the sentence however, is a verb in the imperative (command) form such as 'come!' Instead of a verb, there are merely two pronominal directives: δευρο (hither, or to here) and ἐξω (outwards).

Thus, Christ calls on the human being, but does not command him. That would infer that the activity, which is normally revealed through the verb in the sentence, but which is absent here, must be human. Man must become active, must initiate the next move. Christ, in uttering the words 'Lazarus, outwards to here!' shows the way. This simple, precise observation of the grammatical form's inference leads to discoveries which reveal a new realm of meaning: the co-creating human activity is the prerequisite for divine grace.

The Greek of the New Testament, Koine

In universities and schools, Attic Greek, the dialect that was spoken in Attica which includes Athens, is normally taught. There is, however, also Doric, which appeared for example in the Choir of Greek tragedies; Aeolian of the lyric writings of Sappho and Alcaeus of Mytelene; as well as Ionian, the language in which the philosophic texts of the pre-Socratics and Heraclitus have come down to us. There is therefore no *definitive* Greek language.

The Greek languages have in the course of their three thousand years of history undergone developments, transformations and metamorphoses. Out of written and spoken Attic, the universal language of Koine developed. Koine means 'common', that is, the language spoken by all. In the period roughly spanning 300 BC to AD 600, Koine was the language spoken and written in much of the Mediterranean area. Through the conquering and founding of cities by Alexander the Great, Koine Greek spread further afield to his great Eastern Empire, through Persia, Afghanistan and up until the borders of India. Koine was by no means purely the language of the educated, but also that of the traders, merchants and sailors.

The process of the universal dissemination of this language as *the* foremost means of communication, is astonishing. This language, emanating from a relatively small country, transforms through cultural mingling, connections and semantic creativity to become *the* lingua franca, the language of universal currency of a great part of the world.

Koine is the language of the New Testament and also that of the letters of the Jewish Pharisee and teacher of the Torah, Saul of Tarsus, who, as was common in the Hellenic world, carried a second Greco-Latinised name with which he was to become world-famous, Paul.[2]

The Greek Old Testament: the Septuagint

How potently Koine shaped culture is shown in a particular way by the necessity in the third pre-Christian century to translate the Tanakh, the Hebrew Old Testament, into Greek. The Jews of the Diaspora had become so at home in Koine Greek, that they could no longer understand their own Hebrew Scriptures. So at the time of Ptolemy II (285–246 BC) a Greek translation was instigated, which, according to legend, was completed by 72 Jewish scholars.[3] Hence it was called Septuagint, Latin for seventy. This work became the Bible of the Diaspora Jews and was recited in the synagogue services. When the Old Testament is quoted in the New Testament, it is mostly from the text of the Septuagint. The writers of the gospels needed only to insert this version without translation into their own texts. This led not only to a linguistic unity between the two books of the Bible, but also to a unified sequence of content.

Significant scholars wrote in Koine Greek. For example, the mathematicians Archimedes and Euclid, the historian Polybius, philosophers such as Theophrastus (a pupil of Aristotle), Epicurus and the Stoic Zeno of Citium. It is all the more astonishing then that the Koine Greek of the New Testament is occasionally referred to as 'merely' a popular vernacular, and it is seen as regrettable that Classical Greek was not used. Yet it is precisely the *common* quality of the vernacular that rendered the New Testament accessible to all levels of society. Without this, Christianity might have remained an affair of a small Jewish religious community of Hebrew or Aramaic-speaking peoples.

Ahavah and agapē

The particularly creative power of Septuagint Koine can be well illustrated through an example. A passage in the Song of Songs (8:6): 'for love is strong as death' כי־עזה כמות אהבה *(ki-'azah kamawet ahavah)* created difficulties for a translator, since the word used for love had no corresponding word in Greek. There are a number of words for *to love* or *love* (as verb and noun), such as φιλια *(philia)* love amongst equals, friends; στοργη *(storgē)* caring love, parental love; χαρις *(charis)* favour, popularity, benevolence; ἐρως *(erōs)* the love that discovers the beauty in others and is impassioned by it, a love which embraces the entire human in body, soul, and spirit, and also the love which is the ground upon which all creativity depends.

The Hebrew word אהבה *ahavah* in the above passage from the Song of Songs seemed to have no appropriate equivalent in existing Greek. So the writers of the Septuagint creatively bound together two etymologically related words to form a single whole. From ἀγαπαω *(agapaō)* to love, and ἀγαμαι *(agamai)* to wonder, to revere, there arose a new noun: ἀγαπη *(agapē)*.

And so, when the content of these two words was combined, a translation could be rendered thus: 'to love, to absorb into oneself reverently, something divine, the higher being of the other'.[4]

Through this harmony of etymologically related verbs, a firm foundation was laid for a new noun. This particular form of love could now be expressed in a single word, and not in a lengthy paraphrase. In this manner, the word *agapē* was born. Appropriately, the passage was then translated: κραταια ὡς θανατος ἀγαπη *(krataia hōs thanatos agapē)* 'strong like death, is agapē-love.'

The newly created word *agapē* is today regarded as a particular concept of the New Testament. It is the word for love's apotheosis: God's love for man, man's love for God, and man's love for one another.

Before his Passion, Christ speaks of this love in the High Priestly Prayer: '... that the agapē-love with which you have loved me may be in them, and I in them' (John 17:26). This newly created word is used particularly by St John in his gospel.[5]

Grammar

In his lectures on the Trinity Rudolf Steiner said,

> In former times, one knew that what lives in grammar, what lives in words and contexts, that is something which leads further into Imagination. One knew that the angel was working in such contexts.[6]

Working over the years with texts from the Old and New Testaments has made clear to me time and time again how important a role grammar plays in understanding a gospel text. If we are prepared to see grammar not simply as a body of rules, but as a spiritual creation with its own capacity to give sense, then a text can begin to reveal much deeper levels of meaning than a mere word-for-word translation can offer.

INTRODUCTION

The Greek language has a wealth of grammatical forms. Since English and German are strongly influenced by Latin grammar, it may be useful first to develop a sense for the meaning of some grammatical forms. It is for instance, natural for us to think of a verb in temporal terms, like present, future, past, etc. The emphasis here is on *when* something occurs.

For the Greeks, and especially for the Hebrews of the ancient world this was of lesser significance than *how* something happens. In whose interest and of whose concern is it? Does it occur intensively, repeatedly, punctually? Is it completed or is the matter still open? Was it imagined or real? Or does it express a wish? *How* does it happen?

Such aspects can be expressed in a variety of forms in Greek, which are absent in English.

Whereas in many European languages, we have a duality of grammatical forms, in Greek there are often three. For example, in addition to *active* and *passive,* there is a third form, the *medium* (to do something for oneself, in one's own interest). Besides singular and plural, there is the dual (both). And as well as the indicative (reality) and conjunctive (possibility), there is the optative (wish).

Special mention must be made of the aorist form which is frequently used. The word comes from *ἀ-όρος (a-oros)* without limitation, indefinite, or *ἀ-ώρα (a-hōra)* without time, timeless. How does one translate a sentence with an 'indefinite and timeless' time?

Or how does one work with the profusion of forms of the participle in the texts? In English and German, there are only two, present and past: 'going' and 'gone' and these are used as adjective or adverb, or can even, supplied with an article, become a noun. In Greek there is a plethora of participle forms, and because of that, the language attains an idiosyncratic sentence structure, which can be difficult to translate adequately into modern languages. What binds all the many forms of the participle together however, is that the form of the participle can indicate a state of affairs which are more process-oriented, or are *becoming* or developing. So it is the opposite of a verb form fixed to a person or a time. It indicates what is *open*. And it is precisely this which enables the reader, or listener of the gospel to feel as if directly spoken to in a quite personal way – unusual for a text.

If we add to the range of meanings of words (including sometimes their etymology), the fruits of a study of grammar and its often difficult forms, then the result can be a far more rewarding encounter with a text. The illuminating discoveries we make can enrich this encounter. This book attempts, through the translation and elucidation of certain passages, to demonstrate just this.

Grammar as a being in the seven liberal arts

Right up until the beginning of the Renaissance, grammar was perceived as an *art* that could provide a special significance for the understanding of texts, and in particular the gospels. In classical antiquity the subjects of education were the seven liberal arts (grammar, rhetoric, logic, arithmetic, geometry, astronomy, music), and grammar was the first of the arts.[7] This education was a disciplined path of self development. Its origins can be traced back to antiquity; it was first presented in this form by the Hellenist teacher Marcus Terentius Varro (116–27 BC).[8] It is largely a matter, as the name 'art' suggests, of a practised capacity, and not of an acquired knowledge. These arts became seen as beings in their own right, and were represented as muses or virgins grouped around the Virgin Sophia, the divine wisdom. It was felt that they were nourished through her living stream of inspiration.

The seven arts were introduced into medieval Christian education, which was perceived as a forming of the human soul and spirit, in the early fifth century by Martianus Capella. He was still part of the spiritual and cultural inheritance of late antiquity. His work, *De nuptis Philologiae et Mercurii* (the Marriage of Philology and Mercury) helped to mediate between ancient spirituality and medieval Christian thinking.[9]

On the west portal of Chartres cathedral (built *c*. 1150) com-

INTRODUCTION

The seven liberal arts on the right (south) tympanum of the west portal of Chartres cathedral (built c. 1150).

prising three doors, in the archivolt of the right (south) tympanum there is a representation of these seven liberal arts. They are represented as muses or virgins, as often in book illustrations of the time. They are all connected here with the goddess of wisdom enthroned in the centre, Mary-Sophia. Above the crown of the Mother of God is the hand of God, pointing to the head of Mary. For the aim of education through the seven liberal arts was to come closer to the divine state of wisdom through immersion into and practice of the arts, eventually becoming transformed by them. It is well known that the seven liberal arts were studied and practised at the school of Chartres. Figures from classical times were represented in the archivolt as personifications of each art. These are Aelius Donatus (grammar), Aristotle (logic), and Cicero (rhetoric) for the three arts of the logos, and Boethius (arithmetic), Euclid (geometry), Ptolemy (astronomy) and Pythagoras (music) for the four arts of number.

By relating the arts to their ancient representatives long before the Renaissance, the medieval mind built a bridge to their classical predecessors. This shows how historical developments are based on earlier foundations that are transformed according to the spirit of the times.

Let us look more closely at the representation at Chartres of grammar. We see the figure of a woman in classical dress, comprising an undergarment and a gown, which also covers her head. In her right hand she holds an object that is traditionally seen as a birch. At her feet, we find two small boys. The one sitting on the left is kneeling, his torso bare and his clothing sliding down.

Grammar (detail from Chartres cathedral)

His upward turned face has an open quality. The mouth too, is slightly open. His right hand is held up as if to receive something. The boy on the right, bent slightly forward, is enveloped in his robe. Half of his head is covered by his apparel. As if withdrawn, his head leans to one side and is supported in his right hand. His eyes appear to be closed. Each of the three figures holds an open book in their left hand.

In her ample uprightness the image of Grammar appears to be protecting her two pupils. Her head is bent forward a little as if she was about to rise and open the way through the roundel of the arts. She seems to be saying that the schooling of the soul through all seven liberal arts begins here. Her face and form express mildness and devotion.

Consequently I find it difficult to agree with the usual interpretation that in this representation, Grammar is shown 'with an assiduous and a lazy student', whom she is threatening to cane with the birch.[10] Even if Grammar's bundle of twigs is construed as a birch, looking at the sculpture leaves one with the impression that it is a bundle of still living branches rather than simply an instrument to punish recalcitrant pupils.

Research into symbology also confirms that the supposed birch is in fact a living branch. From classical times through to the Renaissance grammar, as the foundation of education and instruction, was perceived as an intrinsically *living* processes like the growth of a plant. Without grammar, the Tree of Knowledge could not flourish.[11]

The apparently lazy student (lazy because he is placed under the cane?) demonstrates such a degree of devotion in his upturned face, his smiling mouth, and in his receptive, open hand that it is difficult to understand why it is that he has been labelled lazy. Just as frustrating is the view held that the lazy student is pulling the hair of the diligent pupil, and thereby distracting him. Closer observation suggests that it is in fact the *back* of his hand with which he strokes the other's hair. In contrast to this, the so-called assiduous student gives the impression of a deeply pensive pupil. Bent forward, his head supported in his hand in a gesture known since the ancient world, one may ask whether *he* is the one inwardly absent.

What is remarkable is that the two students appear *only* in the depiction of grammar. Could this imply that the learning and practising imperative to this field is to be an example for all *seven* liberal arts? Is the human process of learning meant to be illustrated here? Could the two figures be an indication of a day and night form of learning? If what is learnt is to become an integral part of oneself, then a night's sleep is necessary for this process of receptivity and transformation to take place.

To perceive grammar as a real being is no longer possible for our modern consciousness. However, if we wish to deepen our understanding of a text, especially one from the Bible, then it may be justifiable to esteem grammar once more – if not as a being or muse, at least as an essential component of any translation.

ישב ותרי
כי יעזב א[
ושכל אשר[
אני אה[
לא תקדלו שמ[
בעבד לא האמ[
כי לאתד והג[
לא תא אחד מג[
בנפש סכלים[
הנפש דש[
ליצא נבי שב[
ומרי חת אגם[
בטוב הסא[

קוּמִי
אוֹרִי
כִּי בָא אוֹרֵךְ
וּכְבוֹד יְהוָה
עָלַיִךְ
זָרָח:

כִּי־הִנֵּה
הַחֹשֶׁךְ יְכַסֶּה־אֶרֶץ
וַעֲרָפֶל לְאֻמִּים

וְעָלַיִךְ
יִזְרַח יְהוָה
וּכְבוֹדוֹ
עָלַיִךְ
יֵרָאֶה:

Advent

Human soul, lift up your heart

The prophet's Advent-cry (Isaiah 60:1–2)

You,
Human soul,
Lift up your heart,
Be light,
So that your light comes
And the clarity of the I-am
About you
May shine.

Behold,
There!
Darkness envelops the earth
And clouds overshadow the people.

But about you
Lights up the I-am,
And its shining clarity,
It is beheld
About you.

You,
Human soul,
Lift up your heart,
Be light,
So that your light comes.*

* The repetition of the first sentence is the author's.

The great Jewish prophet Isaiah is recognised as the major herald of the Messiah, the Christ. In the Isenheim Altarpiece, in the Annunciation scene of the angel Gabriel with Mary, Matthias Grünewald painted Isaiah in the top left hand corner, pointing in the opened book to his prophecy.

This text of Isaiah has the character of a hymn. It contains invocation, consolation and a promise of healing. It was first spoken to the people of Israel long ago in 722 BC, at a particularly dark period of Jewish history, during the Assyrian invasion.

But sacred scripture was never thought to be valid only for a particular situation in historical time. One can see this, for example, in the way that the evangelists or Paul use the words of the Old Testament in a lively, diverse and creative fashion, applying it to the human development and to the development of the world. It is also significant how Christ himself does not merely *explain* the words of Isaiah, but enables his listeners to *experience* their transforming power.[1] This imparts a sense of the active life in the word, from which perhaps Origen's method of opening up a text through 'three levels of meaning' is merely a pale reflection.

What is remarkable in our text from Isaiah is how he speaks beyond his own historical context, even speaking to us today. The two commands 'Lift up your heart' (line 3) and 'be light' (line 4) have the character of an awakening appeal to the soul which is not confined to a particular people, time or place.

A particular mention should be made here of the phrase 'human soul', since this is not explicitly stated in the Hebrew text. It is however *implicit* in the two previously mentioned commands or imperatives. These imperatives are feminine (an unknown form in German and English) and refer to a hidden feminine noun. That noun is *nefesh* as indicated by the Jewish translators of the Greek Septuagint who used the word 'Jerusalem'. In both the Old and New Testaments, 'human soul' and 'Jerusalem' were synonymous. (It was in this sense that Meister Eckhardt wrote, 'stand up Jerusalem, and raise yourself'.)

For the Jews this form of deepened active reading is constantly practised. For the text contains no vowels. These must be filled

ADVENT

The prophet Isaiah. Detail from Matthias Grünewald, Isenheim Altarpiece, c. 1513–15.

in by the reader so that words and their contextual meanings reveal themselves only by a continually deepening, replenishing approach to the text. On the other hand, the grammatical rules are so strict and clear that an arbitrary interpretation is impossible.

There are two forms of darkness and two different experiences of light which are spoken of concerning the human soul's encounter with the divine world. These appear to have a timeless quality. In line 10 we hear of 'darkness' חֹשֶׁךְ *(choshekh)*, and of 'overshadowing clouds' עֲרָפֶל *('arafel)*. Of these two forms, the first darkness has a cold quality, and the second, a nebulous quality. According to anthroposophical understanding, these two may be termed Ahrimanic (cold, dark) and Luciferic (obfuscation) forms.

Interwoven with this (as there is no light without darkness), are two forms of light: אוֹר *('or)* and כָּבוֹד *(kevod):* in the text 'your light' (line 5, *'or*) and '*clarity* of the I-am' (line 6, *kevod)*. The first-mentioned, the coming light *('or)*, for the human soul is an inwardly perceptible light, comparable in its quality to the light of the heavenly bodies, the light of the human face, or the light of the eye.[2] We have here an experience of light, which awakens and illuminates, giving direction, so that something can be understood.

The second light quality, the '*clarity* of the I-am' *(kevod)* which shines about the human soul has a different character. Here the soul is surrounded or 'flooded' by the revelation of another world. In the light of other text passages the word *kevod* can also imply the 'glory of God,' 'abundance,' or 'glory of revelation'. The translation of the two qualities of light from Isaiah's Hebrew text in the Greek Septuagint is particularly instructive. They are φως *(phōs)* and δόξα *(doxa)*. It is these very words that appear in the different accounts of the nativity of Matthew and Luke. The revelation of light to the kings, the magi or star-watchers is formulated as φως *(phōs)*. The revelation to the shepherds in the fields is in the form of δόξα *(doxa)*.

A remark should be added to the translation of lines 4 and 5. A common translation is 'shine, for your light is coming.' The conjunction כִּי *(ki)* that is here, can also be a consecutive form 'so that'.³ In the context of the call of Advent, it seems to me evident to convey Isaiah's intention as being 'so that'. The testimony of the prophet, that a raising-up and 'en-*light*-ening' of the soul must occur in order that the divine light may come, accords with the character of the entire hymn.

In line 6 the words כבוד יהוה *(kevod Yahweh)* are translated as 'the clarity of the I-am'. The holy name Yahweh may not be spoken, as it is the highest and most holy. Instead 'Adonai' (Lord) is said. Hence in many translations of the Old Testament Yahweh is translated as 'Lord'. The word comes from the verb היה *(hayah)* meaning 'to live, to exist, to be'. The answer Moses receives at the burning bush when he asks after the name of God (Exod.3:14) is אהיה אשר אהיה *(ehyeh asher ehyeh)*, 'I am the I am' or 'I am what I will be' is related to this verb.

Expanse prepares my soul

The Magnificat of Mary (Luke 1:46–55)

'Magnificat' is the first word of the Latin translation from the original Greek wording of Luke's hymn to Mary: *Magnificat anima mea Dominum* (my soul praises the Lord). Mary answers with this song of praise to her relative Elizabeth's joyful greeting. Both women were with child. Elizabeth had greeted Mary with the words, 'what does this mean for me that the mother of my Lord has come to me? Behold, as the sound of your greeting came to my ears, the babe in my womb leaped for joy.' (Luke 1:43f).

The reply of Mary is the hymn called the Magnificat. Contained within, are quotes from the prophets, and fragments from seven different psalms. From this, one can surmise how profoundly people of this time lived with the holy scriptures. Each day of the

⁴⁶Μεγαλύνει ἡ ψυχή μου τὸν κύριον,
⁴⁷καὶ ἠγαλλίασεν τὸ πνεῦμά μου ἐπὶ τῷ Θεῷ,
τῷ Σωτῆρί μου·
⁴⁸ὅτι ἐπέβλεψεν ἐπὶ τὴν ταπείνωσιν
τῆς δούλης αὐτοῦ·
ἰδοὺ γὰρ
ἀπὸ τοῦ νῦν μακαριοῦσίν με
πᾶσαι αἱ γενεαί·
⁴⁹ὅτι ἐποίησέν μοι
μεγάλα ὁ δυνατός,
καὶ ἅγιον τὸ ὄνομα αὐτοῦ·
⁵⁰καὶ τὸ ἔλεος αὐτοῦ εἰς γενεὰς καὶ γενεὰς
τοῖς φοβουμένοις αὐτόν.
⁵¹Ἐποίησεν κράτος ἐν βραχίονι αὐτοῦ,
διεσκόρπισεν
ὑπερηφάνους διανοίᾳ καρδίας αὐτῶν·
⁵²καθεῖλεν δυνάστας
ἀπὸ θρόνων
καὶ ὕψωσεν ταπεινούς·
⁵³πεινῶντας ἐνέπλησεν ἀγαθῶν
καὶ πλουτοῦντας
ἐξαπέστειλεν κενούς·
⁵⁴ἀντελάβετο Ἰσραὴλ παιδὸς αὐτοῦ,
μνησθῆναι ἐλέους,
⁵⁵καθὼς ἐλάλησεν πρὸς τοὺς πατέρας ἡμῶν,
τῷ Ἀβραὰμ
καὶ τῷ σπέρματι αὐτοῦ, εἰς τὸν αἰῶνα.

entire life of pious Jews was permeated with prayer, psalms and the words of their Scriptures.

So it was, that *Shema Yisrael,* 'Hear, O Israel,' the central prayer from Deuteronomy (6:4–9) of an observing Jew (which Christ also quotes, Mark 12:29) would be whispered into the ear of a new-born child by the father, and were also the last words spoken by or to the dying.

> [46]*Expanse prepares* my soul *for the I am*
> [47]And my spirit it rejoices *in the living one,*
> My saviour
> [48]Because he has turned his vision
> Upon me, *the human being,* in all servility.
> Behold, O soul,
> From the *instant* of understanding
> All generations will call me blessed,
> [49]Because the Mighty One
> Has done great things to me
> And hallowed is his name
> [50]His mercy goes from generation to generation
> To those who hold him in *reverence*
> [51]His arm shows strength
> And *he separates like wheat from the chaff*
> Proud thoughts in their hearts.
> [52]He throws down *those who think themselves mighty,*
> *From the inner throne*
> And raises *that which cannot see itself.*
> [53]Those *who hunger for the spirit,* he fills with good things
> And those who *imagine themselves fulfilled*
> He sent away empty,
> [54]He gives help to his child, *the seeker of God,*
> And remembering mercy,
> [55]As he has said to our fathers,
> To Abraham, the exalted *father of believers*
> And to *the man coming after him* – in aeons.

Beyond being the sublime song of the Mother of God, this hymn may be seen as a call to man, as Angelus Silesius said, 'You must become as Mary, and give birth to God within you.' It is as if Mary speaks for the human soul, which waits expectantly and with great longing for the advent of the divine I am.

Many translations and settings are from the Latin translation of the original Greek text (as we see in the Latin title, *Magnificat*). My translation followed the Greek original. The words in *italics* have a brief commentary below. The length of each line is a conscious attempt to express something of the poetic character of the hymn in a modern European language.

Expanse prepares (verse 46): The hymn begins with the word μεγαλυνει *(megalunei)* which means to make great, to widen. 'Expanse prepares' tries to give an approximation of the meaning and weight of the soul's cry.

The I am and *the living one* (verses 46 and 47): The word κυριος *(kyrios)* and θεος *(theos)* are usually translated as 'the Lord' and 'God'. Since at this point, the hymn quotes Isaiah 61:10 verbatim, I have chosen to replace the somewhat rigid 'Lord' and 'God' with: 'the I am' and 'the living one', as they more closely correspond to the original Hebrew fragment. This leaves the listener freer, giving more space for thoughts and feelings.

The *human being* (verse 48): δουλη *(doulē)* carries the meaning of 'maid, servant'. With the basic premise that Mary speaks on behalf of the human soul, I have translated the line as, 'Upon me, the human being, in all servility.' Mary, whose name Miriam means 'the loving one' and 'the beloved', represents here the image of the human soul which experiences in its innermost self, the God, the I am.

Instant (verse 48): the little word νυν *(nun)* concerns the moment of encounter between the two women, in which the two children 'recognise' each other (Luke 1:44). Transferred to the seeking soul, this would infer: the inner awakening of the self, in awakening to the you of the other. For Greek understanding, this *nun* calls up the flashing moment of great import, the καιρος *(kairos).* The German word *Augenblick* (the blink of an eye, or instant) captures this. This moment is distinct from the usual stream of time χρονος *(chronos).*

To those who hold him in reverence (verse 50): τοις φοβουμενοις αὐτον *(tois phoboumenois auton)* is most often translated as 'those who fear him'. The word φοβεω *(phobeō),* however, has the double meaning of 'to be fearful' as well as 'to revere'. In this sense, one refers to 'God-fearing', and the English word 'awe' has elements of both meanings.

He separates the wheat from the chaff (verse 51): διασκορπιζω *(diaskorpizō)* means to winnow, that is separating the grain from its husk. Applying my interpretation that the individual human soul and not a whole people is the stage of the drama of this assertion, then it also requires a nuance that affects the reader in a different fashion. Within the human soul discernment of the essential from the non-essential is like the winnowing on the threshing floor.

He throws down those who think themselves mighty, from the inner throne / And raises that which cannot see itself (verse 52): καφειλεν δυναστας *(kapheilen dynastas).* Equally, the 'mighty', who are thrown down from the throne, as well as the 'humble', who will be raised (as they are mostly translated), are an image of the human soul. Two perspectives appear here as two temptations, that will be familiar to all: to exaggerate the worth of oneself *(think themselves mighty),* sitting on *'an inner throne',* and to deprecate oneself *(cannot see itself).* Both imply that the subject cannot or will not accept its divine nature.

Those who hunger for the spirit ... And those who imagine themselves fulfilled (verse 53): If, in continuing our understanding of the text in the sense of Angelus Silesius, we examine πεινωντας *(peinōntas,* those who hunger) and πλουτουντας *(ploutountas,* the rich), then we find that it concerns not so much harmonising the social difference between rich and poor, but rather those *who hunger for the spirit,* and those who are *fulfilled* or sated, according to the intensity of their search for the spirit.[4]

The seeker of God (verse 54): I have chosen these words to translate the name Israel that is in the text, because *Isra-el* means 'fighter, champion for El, the living God'. This is the name that Jacob received following his struggle in the night with the angel. Such a warrior is a seeker.

The father of believers (verse 55): The name Abraham signifies 'father of many peoples' (Gen.17:5) and also 'father of believers' (Matt.3:9 and Rom.4:9). As such, he is honoured in Judaism, Islam and Christianity.

And to the man coming after him (verse 56): The text literally states τω σπερματι αὐτου *(tō spermati autou),* 'as God has spoken to Abraham and his seed.' This too can pertain beyond the peoples of Israel to all those who follow an inner path.

A certain peculiarity of the original Greek text is also apparent. Almost all of the verbs are set in the aorist case, the 'timeless' or 'endless' case. I have reproduced it for our modern language in the form of the present. The grammatical use of the aorist emphasises the enduring validity of the text.

Over the centuries, this hymn of Mary has affected many peoples and generations. It is one of the indispensable texts of Christianity. In the Eastern Church it is a key part of the morning prayers, and in the Western Church of evening vespers. The hymn is an essential element in many European songbooks, and is part of the daily prayer of the ecumenical Taizé Community.

It is no surprise that this hymn, full of a powerful melody of speech, is so often translated and set to music. Beginning in the fourteenth century with anonymous musicians, composers such as Vivaldi, Bach, Telemann, Schubert, Mendelssohn, Bartholdy, Bruckner, Tchaikovsky, Arvo Pärt and Steve Dobrogosz (2003) amongst many others, have set the words of this hymn to music. The many varieties of the hymn's interpretation are a testament to its durability.

The words of Angelus Silesius, 'you must become as Mary, and give birth to God within you,' are a possible pathway by which one can begin to apply this magnificent hymn to oneself.

. α .
και μ[
εμου[
πηρ ε[
αυτω[
πηρ ω[
ης ου[
τουτ[
ειεμε[
τονπ[ρ
λυπε[
ματαβ[
. . χζ

Christmas

Magi came from the rising sun

(Matt.2:1–12)

The phenomenon of the star of Bethlehem already occupied minds since the beginnings of Christianity, and was the subject of the most varied astronomical calculations and astrological speculations. It was primarily a question of calculating the precise time of this stellar constellation to anchor it in history. But the appearance of this extraordinary star signified for a writer such as Matthew something different of import. His gospel continually shows the connection between centuries-old prophecies and their fulfilment through Jesus Christ. The star of Bethlehem itself was presaged: Balaam, a Mesopotamian prophet, was given the task by the king of Moab of cursing Israel. However, against his will, his curse transformed itself into a prophetic blessing, and Balaam prophesied a star as the sign for a special King of Israel who was to be expected. The star – mentioned in Matthew 2:2 as that which the 'wise men from the east' follow – was perceived as the valid fulfilment of this prophecy. Balaam had prophesied 'seeing a face of the Almighty, falling prostrate, but having his eyes uncovered: I see him, but not now; I behold him ... a star shall come forth from Jacob' (Num.24:16f).

The three Kings who pay homage and bring gifts to the new-born divine child, are a deep-rooted image in Christian consciousness. In countless representations in painting, sculpture and literature, in legends, plays, crib figures and Christmas carols, they remain alive to this day. The house blessing often found in South Germany and Switzerland, C + M + B (for Caspar,

Melchior, and Balthasar), which is written in chalk over a house door, can be read either as the initials of the three names, or as the abbreviation representing the blessing *Christus mansionem benedicat* (Christ bless this house).

If one looks at the gospel text (Matt 2:1) which is the origin of this colourful and widespread tradition, one may be surprised how little is actually spoken of these so-called three kings. There, we find merely: 'Now when Jesus was born in Bethlehem of Judea during the reign of King Herod, magi (wise ones) arrived from the east.'

There is no mention of kings, none of a triumvirate, and lastly no names either. In the early years of Christianity, in the third century, the magi are first described by Tertullian (150–230) as 'royal'. Three hundred years later, their names appear in one of the most famous mosaics in Saint Apollinaire in Ravenna. Notably, the three names derive from three different cultures:

Balthasar (Babylonian) = God protect life
Melchior (Hebrew) = King of light
Caspar (Persian) = Master of the treasure

The Greek word μαγοι *(magoi)*, which appears in Matthew, does not mean king, but rather astronomer, and was in this sense also mentioned by Herodotus, Strabo and Philo. All three scholars refer to a Median priestly caste of magi. These representatives of the Zoroastrian religion were physicians, priests and astrologers. The Zoroastrian magi awaited the return of the great Zarathustra.

Rudolf Steiner said, 'What illuminates the path of the magi is nothing less than the soul of Christ itself.'[1]

Τοῦ δὲ Ἰησοῦ γεννηθέντος ἐν Βηθλέεμ τῆς Ἰουδαίας
ἐν ἡμέραις Ἡρῴδου τοῦ βασιλέως,
ἰδοὺ
μάγοι ἀπὸ ἀνατολῶν παρεγένοντο εἰς Ἱεροσόλυμα
²λέγοντες·
Ποῦ ἐστιν ὁ τεχθεὶς βασιλεὺς τῶν Ἰουδαίων;
εἴδομεν γὰρ αὐτοῦ τὸν ἀστέρα ἐν τῇ ἀνατολῇ,
καὶ ἤλθομεν προσκυνῆσαι αὐτῷ·
³ἀκούσας δὲ ὁ βασιλεὺς Ἡρῴδης ἐταράχθη,
καὶ πᾶσα Ἱεροσόλυμα μετ᾽ αὐτοῦ,
⁴καὶ συναγαγὼν πάντας τοὺς ἀρχιερεῖς
καὶ γραμματεῖς τοῦ λαοῦ
ἐπυνθάνετο παρ᾽ αὐτῶν ποῦ ὁ Χριστὸς γεννᾶται·
⁵οἱ δὲ εἶπαν αὐτῷ· Ἐν Βηθλέεμ τῆς Ἰουδαίας·
οὕτως γὰρ γέγραπται διὰ τοῦ προφήτου·
⁶Καὶ σύ Βηθλέεμ, γῆ Ἰούδα,
οὐδαμῶς ἐλαχίστη εἶ ἐν τοῖς ἡγεμόσιν Ἰούδα·
ἐκ σοῦ γὰρ ἐξελεύσεται ἡγούμενος,
ὅστις ποιμανεῖ τὸν λαόν μου τὸν Ἰσραήλ.
⁷Τότε Ἡρῴδης, λάθρα καλέσας τοὺς μάγους
ἠκρίβωσεν παρ᾽ αὐτῶν
τὸν χρόνον τοῦ φαινομένου ἀστέρος,
⁸καὶ πέμψας αὐτοὺς εἰς Βηθλέεμ, εἶπεν·
Πορευθέντες ἐξετάσατε ἀκριβῶς περὶ τοῦ παιδίου,
ἐπὰν δὲ εὕρητε, ἀπαγγείλατέ μοι,
ὅπως κἀγώ ἐλθών, προσκυνήσω αὐτῷ·
⁹οἱ δὲ ἀκούσαντες τοῦ βασιλέως ἐπορεύθησαν·
καὶ ἰδοὺ ὁ ἀστήρ, ὃν εἶδον
ἐν τῇ ἀνατολῇ,
προῆγεν αὐτούς ἕως ἐλθών, ἐστάθη ἐπάνω οὗ ἦν τὸ
    παιδίον·
¹⁰ἰδόντες δὲ τὸν ἀστέρα
ἐχάρησαν χαρὰν μεγάλην σφόδρα·
¹¹καὶ ἐλθόντες εἰς τὴν οἰκίαν, εἶδον τὸ παιδίον μετὰ
    Μαρίας
τῆς μητρὸς αὐτοῦ,

Now Jesus having been born in Bethlehem in Judea
In the days of Herod the King,
Behold,
Magi came from the rising sun to Jerusalem
²And they spoke:
'Where is the new-born, the King of the Jews?
We have seen his star, in the East
And have come to worship him.'
³Hearing this, Herod was deeply troubled
And all Jerusalem with him;
⁴He called all the High Priests
And scribes of the people to him
And inquired from them, where the Christ was to be born.
⁵Now they spoke to him: 'In Bethlehem, in Judea,
For it is written in the prophets
⁶"And you Bethlehem, in the land of Judah,
Are not the least of the towns of Judah
For out of you shall come the ruler
Who will shepherd my people Israel".'
⁷Herod secretly called the magi to him
And inquired of them
The time of the appearance of the star
⁸And he sent them to Bethlehem and said:
'Go and ask carefully after the child
And when you have found it, so tell me
So that I can go and worship too.'
⁹As they heard this, they took their way
And behold, the star, that they had seen
In the east
Led them until having come, it stood over above the
    child
¹⁰And they beheld the star
And rejoiced greatly in tremendous joy
¹¹And going into the house, and seeing the child with
    Mary,
His mother,

καὶ πεσόντες προσεκύνησαν αὐτῷ,
καὶ ἀνοίξαντες τοὺς θησαυροὺς αὐτῶν προσήνεγκαν
    αὐτῷ δῶρα,
χρυσὸν καὶ λίβανον καὶ σμύρναν·
¹²καὶ χρηματισθέντες κατ᾽ ὄναρ
μὴ ἀνακάμψαι πρὸς Ἡρῴδην,
δι᾽ ἄλλης ὁδοῦ ἀνεχώρησαν εἰς τὴν χώραν αὐτῶν.

Ἐγένετο δὲ ἐν ταῖς ἡμέραις ἐκείναις
ἐξῆλθεν δόγμα παρά Καίσαρος Αὐγούστου
ἀπογράφεσθαι
πᾶσαν τὴν οἰκουμένην·
²αὕτη ἀπογραφὴ πρώτη
ἐγένετο ἡγεμονεύοντος τῆς Συρίας Κυρηνίου·
³καὶ ἐπορεύοντο πάντες ἀπογράφεσθαι,
ἕκαστος εἰς τὴν ἑαυτοῦ πόλιν.
⁴Ἀνέβη δὲ καὶ Ἰωσὴφ ἀπὸ τῆς Γαλιλαίας ἐκ πόλεως
    Ναζαρέθ
εἰς τὴν Ἰουδαίαν εἰς πόλιν Δαυὶδ ἥτις καλεῖται Βηθλέεμ,
διὰ τὸ εἶναι αὐτὸν ἐξ οἴκου καὶ πατριᾶς Δαυίδ,
⁵ἀπογράψασθαι σὺν Μαριὰμ τῇ ἐμνηστευμένῃ αὐτῷ,
οὔσῃ ἐγκύῳ.
⁶Ἐγένετο δὲ ἐν τῷ εἶναι αὐτοὺς ἐκεῖ
ἐπλήσθησαν αἱ ἡμέραι τοῦ τεκεῖν αὐτήν,
⁷Καὶ ἔτεκεν τὸν υἱὸν αὐτῆς τὸν πρωτότοκον,

CHRISTMAS

> And they bent down,
> Opened their treasures brought forth their gifts:
> Gold and incense and myrrh.
> ¹²But in a dream it was revealed to them
> Not to return to Herod,
> So they departed on another way back to their land.*

And shepherds were in this land (Luke 2:1–20)

Let us turn now to the other nativity story, as related by Luke. This is the narrative which is customarily read in churches at Christmas. This version is held in Central Europe to be the main Christmas story.

> And it happened in those days,
> That there came a decree from the Caesar Augustus
> That for taxing a census should take place
> Of the whole world.
> ²And this census was the first and happened
> As Quirinius was governor of Syria
> ³And all were travelling on the way
> Each to his town.
> ⁴Joseph too left Galilee, from the town of Nazareth
> To go to Judea, to the city of David, which is called Bethlehem
> As he was of the house of David and was of his lineage
> ⁵To register himself with Mary, his wife.
> She was pregnant.
> ⁶Now it happened, as they were there,
> That the days of the birth were fulfilled
> ⁷And she bore her son, the first-born

---

* The Old Testament quotations in verse 6 refer to Isa.7:42, and also to Mic.5:1,3; 2Sam.5:2; 1Chr.11:2.

καὶ ἐσπαργάνωσεν αὐτὸν
καὶ ἀνέκλινεν αὐτὸν ἐν φάτνῃ,
διότι οὐκ ἦν αὐτοῖς τόπος ἐν τῷ καταλύματι.
⁸Καὶ ποιμένες ἦσαν ἐν τῇ χώρᾳ τῇ αὐτῇ
ἀγραυλοῦντες
καὶ φυλάσσοντες φυλακὰς τῆς νυκτὸς ἐπὶ τὴν ποίμνην αὐτῶν·
⁹καὶ ἄγγελος Κυρίου ἐπέστη αὐτοῖς
καὶ δόξα Κυρίου περιέλαμψεν αὐτούς,
καὶ ἐφοβήθεσαν φόβον μέγαν·
¹⁰καὶ εἶπεν αὐτοῖς ὁ ἄγγελος· Μὴ φοβεῖσθε·
ἰδοὺ γὰρ εὐαγγελίζομαι ὑμῖν χαρὰν μεγάλην,
ἥτις ἔσται παντὶ τῷ λαῷ,
¹¹ὅτι ἐτέχθη ὑμῖν σήμερον Σωτήρ,
ὅς ἐστιν Χριστὸς Κύριος, ἐν πόλει Δαυίδ·
¹²καὶ τοῦτο ὑμῖν τὸ σημεῖον,
εὑρήσετε βρέφος
ἐσπαργανωμένον
καὶ κείμενον ἐν φάτνῃ·
¹³καὶ εξαίφνης ἐγένετο σὺν τῷ ἀγγέλῳ
πλῆθος στρατιᾶς οὐρανίου
αἰνούντων τὸν Θεὸν, καὶ λεγόντων·
¹⁴Δόξα ἐν ὑψίστοις Θεῷ
καὶ ἐπὶ γῆς εἰρήνη
ἐν ἀνθρώποις εὐδοκίας.
¹⁵Καὶ ἐγένετο, ὡς ἀπῆλθον ἀπ' αὐτῶν εἰς τὸν οὐρανὸν οἱ ἄγγελοι,
οἱ ποιμένες ἐλάλουν πρὸς ἀλλήλους·
Διέλθωμεν δὴ ἕως Βηθλέεμ
καὶ ἴδωμεν τὸ ῥῆμα τοῦτο τὸ γεγονὸς
ὃ ὁ Κύριος ἐγνώρισεν ἡμῖν·
¹⁶καὶ ἦλθαν σπεύσαντες, καὶ ἀνεῦραν τήν τε Μαριὰμ καὶ τὸν Ἰωσὴφ
καὶ τὸ βρέφος κείμενον ἐν τῇ φάτνῃ·
¹⁷ἰδόντες δὲ ἐγνώρισαν περὶ
τοῦ ῥήματος
τοῦ λαληθέντος αὐτοῖς περὶ τοῦ παιδίου τούτου·

And she wrapped him in cloths
And laid him in a manger
As there was no room at the inn.
[8]And there were shepherds in this land,
Living under the clear skies
And watching, protecting their herds at night.
[9]And the angel of God came forth to them
And the glory of God shone around them
And they were terribly overcome with fear
[10]And there spoke to them the Angel: 'Do not fear
For behold, I announce to you great joy,
Which will be for all people:
[11]Born to you today is the Saviour
Who is God's Christ, in the city of David.
[12]And this will be a sign for you:
You will find a small infant
Wrapped in cloths, and resting at the place
Where one ties up the animal in a stable.'
[13]And suddenly, with the angel
A multitude of the company of the heavens
That praised God and sang:
[14]'Glory in the highest to God
And over the earth peace
Among men of *good will.*'
[15]And it happened that the angels went from them to the heavens
And the shepherds spoke to one another:
'Let us go up to Bethlehem
And see this word, that has happened,
That God has revealed to us.'
[16]And they came hastily, and they found Mary and Joseph
And the infant, resting at a place
[17]And they perceived it and they made known
The word
That was said to them by this child.

¹⁸καὶ πάντες οἱ ἀκούσαντες ἐθαύμασαν
περὶ τῶν λαληθέντων ὑπὸ τῶν ποιμένων πρὸς αὐτούς·
¹⁹ἡ δὲ Μαρία πάντα συνετήρει τὰ ῥήματα ταῦτα
συμβάλλουσα ἐν τῇ καρδίᾳ αὐτῆς·
²⁰καὶ ὑπέστρεψαν οἱ ποιμένες
δοξάζοντες καὶ αἰνοῦντες τὸν Θεὸν
ἐπὶ πᾶσιν οἷς ἤκουσαν καὶ εἶδον
καθὼς ἐλαλήθη πρὸς αὐτούς.

> ¹⁸And all that heard it, were astonished about that
> Which was told to them by the shepherds.
> ¹⁹But Mary kept all these words
> And moved them in her heart.
> ²⁰And the shepherds turned back
> Praising and glorifying God for everything
> That they had heard and seen –
> Just as it was said to them.

We commonly take elements from the two narratives of Luke and Matthew, and see them in chronological order. For example, first, the shepherds, then the kings betake themselves on the journey to worship the child. Taking a step back from our habitual view, however, we first notice how the two narratives evidently contradict each other, and can make several surprising discoveries.

If we compare the two genealogies (Matt.1:1 and Luke 3:1) we may be astonished that, despite several common features, we are actually faced with two very different genealogies. The one lineage runs through the son of David, King Solomon. The second catalogue of names passes through the priest Nathan, another of David's sons. The divergence is indubitable. Even the named grandfathers of Jesus are inconsistent. The problem of the discrepancies in the two family trees was a point of discussion from the beginnings of the Church. The early Church Fathers such as Ignatius of Antioch, Irenaeus, and Justin Martyr and others had already extensively analysed this quandary.[2] Since this question has even today remained apparently insoluble, we are left with the curious conclusion that the genealogies are purely fictive.

But there are further important contrasts.

In Luke, *only* the shepherds are mentioned. In Matthew, *only* the magi.

In Luke, the revelation to the shepherds is effected through the *word of the angel.* In Matthew, it is through the manifestation of a *star script.*

In Luke, the encounter with the angelic world releases an elemental terror, or fear *(φοβος, phobos)* in the shepherds.

In Matthew, the magi's successful deciphering of the star script leads to a thrice emphasised *overwhelming joy: ἐχαρεσεν χαραν μεγαλαν, σφοδρα (echaresen charan megalan sphodra)* 'they rejoiced greatly with tremendous joy.' Nowhere do we hear of fear.

The place where Mary, Joseph and the child are found in the Gospel of Luke (2:7) is the καταλυμα *(kataluma),* the simple refuge for shepherds and wayfarers with animals. Or rather, as there was no place at this refuge, in a φατνη *(phatnē),* a manger, or as in one recognised text variant, ἐν τω σπηλαιω φατνη *(en tō spēlaiō phatnē),* a cave, or grotto in which animals are lodged.

In comparison, we find in Matthew no mention of a cave or stable. The three magi find the child together with his mother in an οἶκος *(oikos),* which is in fact, a proper *house.*

It is also remarkable that the way the shepherds and magi perceive of the birth differs. In the speech of the shepherds, Luke (2:15) uses 'that God has *revealed* to us,' ἐγνωρισεν *(egnōrisen),* denoting a form of cognition of which the word 'gnosis' is an integral part.

The corresponding passage of Matthew (2:2) reads εἰδομεν γαρ τον ἀστερα *(eidomen gar ton astera),* 'we have seen a star.' In *eidomen* we have the word 'idea'.

The two texts differentiate quite clearly between the two forms of knowledge. On the one hand, a somewhat intuitive vision, deeply connected with nature and cosmos which the shepherds manifest. Under exceptional circumstances, they are capable of perceiving the δοξα *(doxa),* the light, the splendour, the appearance of revelation from another world.[3] Another way is through the schooling of acquired knowledge and uniting phenomena *in the idea,* as befits the star-sages, the magi.

Further examination of the incongruities reveals the contextual dissonance between the two narratives. In Luke, Mary and Joseph were residents of Nazareth who journeyed to Bethlehem for the census. After eight days they had their child circumcised, and later, after forty days in accord with the Law (Exod 13:2), they 'presented the first-born' in the Temple. Here, the child was blessed by Hannah and Simeon. Luke remains silent about Herod's slaughter of the children and the flight to Egypt.

In contrast, Matthew does not mention Nazareth as the dwelling of the parents. They are residents of Bethlehem, where their child is born, and from where they flee to Egypt. Here they remain until the danger has subsided. In a dream, Joseph is told that they should not return to Bethlehem, but rather should settle in Nazareth in Galilee.

In reviewing the evident incongruities in the two narratives as a whole, the question may justifiably be raised as to whether the texts actually chronicle *two different children.* This inquiry acquired tremendous controversy in 1947 when the Qumran Scrolls were discovered in the Judean Desert. The Essene documents found there revealed that *two* different Messiah figures were clearly expected: one priestly in essence, the other, of royal character.[4] When these texts were first analysed, experts (for example, Kurt Schubert) believed that they were dealing with a scribal error. Such an idea appeared to be incompatible with what was known of Jewish as well as Christian tradition.[5] Three years later, however, Schubert had to revise his earlier thesis on account of the plenitude of references to an expected *two* messiahs, one priestly, one kingly.[6] The theory of a 'slip of the pen' was no longer tenable. Since then, the teaching of the two Messiahs as found in the Essene annals, has on the grounds of its own evidence, become universally recognised.[7] Following this acknowledgment, it became possible to 'discover' other passages in the Old Testament which implied such a duality. Here, we may remind ourselves of the old axiom: one can only see that which one can think.

Thus we find for example, an extract in Zechariah (4:3–14) in which the prophet asks,

> 'What do these two olive trees mean, one on the right, the other on the left of candelabra?' ... He said to me, 'You do not know what they are?' I said, 'No, Adonai.' He said, 'Those are the *two messiahs,* who stand before the Lord of the whole earth.'

15 וַיִּשָּׂא מְשָׁלוֹ וַיֹּאמַר
נְאֻם בִּלְעָם בְּנוֹ בְעֹר
וּנְאֻם הַגֶּבֶר שְׁתֻם הָעָיִן:
16 נְאֻם שֹׁמֵעַ אִמְרֵי־אֵל
וְיֹדֵעַ דַּעַת עֶלְיוֹן
מַחֲזֵה שַׁדַּי
יֶחֱזֶה נֹפֵל וּגְלוּי עֵינָיִם:
17 אֶרְאֶנּוּ וְלֹא עַתָּה
אֲשׁוּרֶנּוּ וְלֹא קָרוֹב
דָּרַךְ כּוֹכָב מִיַּעֲקֹב
וְקָם שֵׁבֶט מִיִּשְׂרָאֵל

Another passage in Zechariah (6:11–13) explicitly addresses the ministerial and royal elements: 'He will build a temple of the Lord, and shall bear *royal* honour, and shall sit upon his throne. And there shall be a priest by his throne, and peaceful understanding shall be between them both.'

In 1909, almost forty years before the discovery of the Qumran Scrolls, Rudolf Steiner had spoken about two Jesus children, priestly and royal, which his spiritual research had revealed.[8] Such a statement was somewhat disconcerting at the time, and seemingly unverifiable. Steiner's assertion concerning the two Messiahs today appears to be justifiable, considering the purport of the Essene scriptures and the concomitant new exegesis of several prophetic passages in the Old Testament that has inevitably followed.

Similarly, such a duality could also be indicated by the symbolic terms *star* and *sceptre*. The prophecy of Balaam quoted at the beginning of the chapter, reads as follows (Num.24:15–17). Balaam uses three different names for the highest divine being (the Hebrew names are added in italics).

> [15]And he took up his discourse and spoke:
> 'Saying of Balaam, the son of Beor
> Saying of the strong one whose eye is opened
> [16]Saying of the one hearing the words of God *(El)*
> And the one knowing the knowledge of the Most High *('Elyon)*
> Seeing the vision of the Almighty *(Shadai)*
> Falling down, but with eyes uncovered:
> [17]I see him, but not now
> I behold him, but not yet nigh;
> A *star* shall come forth out of Jacob
> And a *sceptre* shall rise out of Israel'

³Ἀφῆκεν τὴν Ἰουδαίαν
καὶ ἀπῆλθεν πάλιν εἰς τὴν Γαλιλαίαν.
⁴Ἔδει δὲ αὐτὸν διέρχεσθαι διὰ τῆς Σαμαρείας·
⁵ἔρχεται οὖν εἰς πόλιν τῆς Σαμαρείας λεγομένην Σύχαρ,
πλησίον τοῦ χωρίου ὃ ἔδωκεν Ἰακὼβ τῷ Ἰωσὴφ τῷ υἱῷ
αὐτοῦ·
⁶ἦν δὲ ἐκεῖ πηγὴ τοῦ Ἰακώβ·
ὁ οὖν Ἰησοῦς κεκοπιακὼς ἐκ τῆς ὁδοιπορίας
ἐκαθέζετο οὕτως ἐπὶ τῇ πηγῇ·

Between Epiphany and Passiontide

I, I am he who speaks with you

*Christ and the woman from Samaria
(John 4:3–26)*

The story of the birth of Jesus according to Luke ends with the words, 'But Mary kept all these words and moved them in her heart' (2:19). With these two activities of the soul – 'keeping' and 'moving' – a theme is touched on which, in a metamorphosed form surfaces again in the story of Christ and the woman at Jacob's well.

The woman comes from the religious group of the Samaritans, who consider themselves to be the 'keepers' of the old Judaic religion (this in fact is the meaning of the name *Shamerim*, Samarian). In her encounter with Christ she is led from 'keeping' to 'moving', to the question of the inner impetus, the inner well of 'living water' in man. In this passage the aorist, the timeless tense, is consciously rendered into the present tense.

> ³Jesus now left the land of Judea
> And went once more forth to Galilee
> ⁴And it was necessary for him to pass through Samaria
> ⁵He came to a town of Samaria, by the name of Sychar,
> Near to the fields that Jacob had given to his son Joseph.
> ⁶Now there was a well of Jacob.
> Since Jesus was now tired from walking
> He sat down at the well.

ὥρα ἦν ὡς ἕκτη·
⁷ἔρχεται γυνὴ ἐκ τῆς Σαμαρείας ἀντλῆσαι ὕδωρ·
λέγει αὐτῇ ὁ Ἰησοῦς·
Δός μοι πεῖν·
⁸οἱ γὰρ μαθηταὶ αὐτοῦ ἀπεληλύθεισαν εἰς τὴν πόλιν,
ἵνα τροφὰς ἀγοράσωσιν·
⁹λέγει οὖν αὐτῷ ἡ γυνὴ ἡ Σαμαρῖτις·
Πῶς σὺ Ἰουδαῖος ὢν παρ' ἐμοῦ πεῖν αἰτεῖς
γυναικὸς Σαμαρίτιδος οὔσης;
οὐ γὰρ συνχρῶνται Ἰουδαῖοι
Σαμαρίταις·
¹⁰ἀπεκρίθη Ἰησοῦς καὶ εἶπεν αὐτῇ·
Εἰ ᾔδεις τὴν δωρεὰν τοῦ Θεοῦ,
καὶ τίς ἐστιν ὁ λέγων σοι· Δός μοι πεῖν,
σὺ ἂν ᾔτησας αὐτὸν
καὶ ἔδωκεν ἄν σοι ὕδωρ ζῶν·
¹¹λέγει αὐτῷ ἡ γυνή·
Κύριε, οὔτε ἄντλημα ἔχεις
καὶ τὸ φρέαρ ἐστὶν βαθύ,
πόθεν οὖν ἔχεις τὸ ὕδωρ τὸ ζῶν;
¹²μὴ σὺ μείζων εἶ τοῦ πατρὸς ἡμῶν Ἰακώβ,
ὅς ἔδωκεν ἡμῖν τὸ φρέαρ,
καὶ αὐτὸς ἐξ αὐτοῦ ἔπιεν
καὶ οἱ υἱοὶ αὐτοῦ καὶ τὰ θρέμματα αὐτοῦ;
¹³ἀπεκρίθη Ἰησοῦς καὶ εἶπεν αὐτῇ·
Πᾶς ὁ πίνων ἐκ τοῦ ὕδατος τούτου,
διψήσει πάλιν·
¹⁴ὃς δ' ἂν πίῃ ἐκ τοῦ ὕδατος
οὗ ἐγὼ δώσω αὐτῷ,
οὐ μὴ διψήσει εἰς τὸν αἰῶνα,
ἀλλὰ τὸ ὕδωρ ὃ δώσω αὐτῷ
γενήσεται ἐν αὐτῷ πηγὴ ὕδατος
ἁλλομένου εἰς ζωὴν αἰώνιον·
¹⁵λέγει πρὸς αὐτὸν ἡ γυνή·
Κύριε, δός μοι τοῦτο τὸ ὕδωρ, ἵνα μὴ διψῶ
μηδὲ διέρχωμαι ἐνθάδε ἀντλεῖν·

It was at the *sixth hour.*
⁷There came a woman from Samaria to draw water.
Jesus says to her:
Give me to drink.
⁸For his disciples had gone into the town
To buy provisions.
⁹Now the Samaritan woman speaks to him:
How can you ask me for something to drink
When you are a Jew, and I a Samaritan woman?
For the Jews have no association
With the Samaritans
¹⁰Jesus answers and says to her:
If you knew the gift of God
And who it is, who says to you: Give me to drink,
You would ask him
And he would give living water.
¹¹The woman says to him:
Lord, you have no bucket
And the well is deep.
From where do you have the living water?
¹²Are you greater than our father Jacob,
Who gave us the well?
And he himself drank from it
And his children and his cattle.
¹³Jesus answers and says to her:
Whoever drinks of this water
Will thirst again;
¹⁴Whoever drinks from the water
That I shall give him
They will eternally not thirst
And the water that I shall give him
Will become in him a spring of water
Welling up as a source of life.
¹⁵The woman says to him:
Lord, give me this water, so that I do not thirst
And I must not come out again to draw water.

¹⁶λέγει αὐτῇ·
Ὕπαγε, φώνησον τὸν ἄνδρα σου καὶ ἐλθὲ ἐνθάδε·
¹⁷ἀπεκρίθη ἡ γυνὴ καὶ εἶπεν αὐτῷ·
Οὐκ ἔχω ἄνδρα·
λέγει αὐτῇ ὁ Ἰησοῦς·
Καλῶς εἶπας ὅτι Ἄνδρα ουκ ἔχω·
¹⁸πέντε γὰρ ἄνδρας ἔσχες, καὶ νῦν ὃν ἔχεις
οὐκ ἔστιν σου ἀνήρ·
τοῦτο ἀληθὲς εἴρηκας·
¹⁹λέγειν αὐτῷ ἡ γυνή· Κύριε, θεωρῶ
ὅτι προφήτης εἶ σύ·
²⁰οἱ πατέρες ἡμῶν ἐν τῷ ὄρει
τούτῳ προσεκύνησαν·
καὶ ὑμεῖς λέγετε ὅτι ἐν Ἱεροσολύμοις ἐστὶν ὁ τόπος
ὅπου προσκυνεῖν δεῖ·
²¹λέγει αὐτῇ ὁ Ἰησοῦς· Πίστευέ μοι, γύναι,
ὅτι ἔρχεται ὥρα, ὅτε οὔτε ἐν τῷ ὄρει τούτῳ
οὔτε ἐν Ἱεροσολύμοις προσκυνήσετε τῷ Πατρί·
²²ὑμεῖς προσκυνεῖτε ὅ οὐκ οἴδατε,
ἡμεῖς προσκυνοῦμεν ὅ οἴδαμεν,
ὅτι ἡ σωτηρία ἐκ τῶν Ἰουδαίων ἐστίν·
²³ἀλλὰ ἔρχεται ὥρα καὶ νῦν ἐστιν,
ὅτε οἱ ἀληθινοὶ προσκυνηταὶ προσκυνήσουσιν τῷ Πατρὶ
ἐν πνεύματι καὶ ἀληθείᾳ·
καὶ γὰρ ὁ Πατὴρ τοιούτους ζητεῖ τοὺς προσκυνοῦντας
　　αὐτόν·
²⁴πνεῦμα ὁ Θεός,
καὶ τοὺς προσκυνοῦντας αὐτὸν
ἐν πνεύματι καὶ ἀληθείᾳ δεῖ προσκυνεῖν·
²⁵λέγει αὐτῷ ἡ γυνή·
Οἶδα ὅτι Μεσσίας ἔρχεται, ὁ λεγόμενος Χριστός,
ὅταν ἔλθῃ ἐκεῖνος, ἀναγγελεῖ ἡμῖν ἅπαντα·
²⁶λέγει αὐτῇ ὁ Ἰησοῦς· Ἐγώ εἰμι,
ὁ λαλῶν σοι.

¹⁶Jesus says to her: Go,
Call your husband and come here.
¹⁷The woman answers and says to him:
I have no husband.
Jesus says to her:
You are right when you say: I have no husband.
¹⁸*Five husbands have you had, and he who you now have*
Is not your husband,
This you have said truly.
¹⁹The woman says to him: Lord, I perceive,
You, you are a prophet.
²⁰On this mountain our fathers
Have worshipped kneeling
And you say that in Jerusalem is the place
Where one should worship
²¹Jesus says to her: Believe me woman,
There is a time coming, when neither on this mountain
Nor in Jerusalem, will the Father be worshipped.
²²You know not what you worship;
We know however, what we worship;
For salvation is coming from the Jews.
²³But a time is coming and it is already upon us,
When the true worshipper will worship the Father
In spirit and in truth;
For also the Father longs for such worshippers.
²⁴God is spirit
And those who worship him
Must worship him in spirit and in truth.
²⁵The woman speaks to him:
I know that the Messiah is coming, he who is called the Christ.
When he comes he will reveal all to us.
²⁶Jesus says to her: *I, I am,*
The one speaking with you.

In order to understand certain aspects of the conversation between Jesus and the woman of Samaria at the well, it is necessary to know something of the history of the Jews and Samaritans.

The Samaritans are often mentioned in the Old and New Testaments. The well-known example is the story of the Good Samaritan (Luke 10:30–37).

In the Second Book of Kings (17:24), the story of the original enmity between Jews and Samaritans is recorded. After the death of King Solomon, the kingdom began to decline (925 BC) and was divided into a southern domain with the capital at Jerusalem, and a northern kingdom, with the capital at Shechem, an important city often mentioned in the Old Testament.[1] In 721 BC, a large part of the Israelite population was deported, leaving a segment in Samaria which swiftly mixed with the five foreign races which had been resettled there by their Assyrian conquerors. In this way, five foreign gods came into Samaria.[2] The deeply mutual contempt and animosity which marked the estrangement between Jews and Samaritans began at this time.

When in 538 BC the Jewish people were permitted under the Persian King Cyrus the Great to return from their Babylonian exile they rebuilt the Temple in Jerusalem under their leader Zerubbabbel.[3] They refused the help of the Samaritans, since they were deemed to be impure, as the mingling with foreign races, cultures and religious cults in Samaria was anathema to the Jews. In their eyes the Samaritans' bond with Yahweh was broken.

In contrast, the Samaritan people felt themselves to be, as their name 'keepers' suggests, the true vessel in which the original form of the Israelite religion was conserved. They only acknowledged therefore the Torah, the five Books of Moses, as the Holy Scriptures, and rejected the later additions to the Old Testament which arose during the Exile.

As their offer of help to rebuild the Temple had been rejected, they proceeded to build their own temple on Mount Gerizim, which was a holy place, for here the people of Israel had been blessed in the days of Joshua (Josh.8:33).[4]

From this outline of the historical background of the common origin and later animosity between these two peoples, the question of the Samaritan woman to Christ concerning the appropriate place of true worship, begins to have a wider meaning.

In what follows, I should like to limit myself to short parts from the text that are printed in italics. These interpretations appear to me important in order to touch on the deeper levels of the text. The method of Origen is retained, which proves to helpfully discriminate between levels of meaning, making them more transparent.

But a time is coming and it is already upon us, when the true worshipper will worship the Father in spirit and in truth for also the Father longs for such worshippers. (Verse 23)

Such is Christ's answer to the question of the Samaritan woman as to where the proper place of worship is. The question had addressed the ancient dispute between Jews and Samaritans, whether the 'correct place' of worship be the Temple of Jerusalem, or Mount Gerizim. Christ's reply opens up an expanse to counteract the constricting nature of the question. He elaborates in three ways: he explains that for the future, beginning in that very moment, the place must be unimportant (verse 21). Further, he speaks of a new form of worshipper, who invokes 'in spirit and in truth.' And he makes clear that the Father also 'longs' for such worship. Here the verb in Greek is ζητεω *(zēteō)* which not only means 'demands, requires', as it is so often translated, but can also mean 'seeks' and 'longs for.'

In this threefold proclamation, the ancient contention concerning the 'right' place is dissolved, and our vision is directed toward the importance of the one who invokes, and a new *striving* form of inner religious life. Besides, we find that the traditional notion of prayer and worship is turned around. Christ says that not only does man long for God – but that God, the divine world, needs, seeks and longs for man.

It was at the sixth hour (Verse 6): In another story about a well from the Old Testament, it is said that it was 'around evening at the time when women come out to fetch water' (Gen.24:11).

Eliezer, Abraham's proxy and go-between for his son Isaac, meets Rebecca in the evening, the usual time of fetching water, by Nahor's well. In comparison, the expressly stated 'sixth hour' surprises us. This is because it is the midday hour, the hottest time of the day. No one from this culture would make their way to fetch water at this time of day.

Additionally, the gospel passage immediately following, includes another detail of time, that is not entirely understandable on a superficial level. When Christ speaks of the cornfields to the disciples, they are said to be 'ripe, and ready for the harvest' (John 4:35). However, the harvest is described as being still four months away. This demonstrates that the external details of the time of day, or year can show aspects of the text transcending time, as we find in this passage in its initial section.

Five husbands you have had (Verse 18): This sentence has been the subject of much interpretation.[5] The proposal by Rudolf Schnackenburg, that it concerns 'the moral degeneracy of (the) woman', and 'her embarrassing fact' of 'five husbands' appears to miss the complexity, mood and content of the encounter.[6]

A key to a more profound understanding of this cardinal sentence is, in my opinion, to be found in the frequently observable change of perspective and levels of communication.

The request, with which the text begins, made by Christ to the nameless Samaritan women for something to drink, turns swiftly to the pronouncement that it is not *he* that should ask *her* for water, but rather she that should ask him for 'living water'. It becomes clear that we are not dealing with differing types of water, with well or spring water, as one might at first think, but rather that the expression 'living water' points to something else. And this seems to be comprehensible to the woman out of her religious background. The term 'living water' was not only understood as spring water, but also since the Babylonian exile, as the Torah and its inherent spiritual power.[7]

One may suppose that the Samaritan woman first understood Christ's speech about the 'living water' to refer to the tradition of the Torah. Nonetheless, her astonished reply, 'From where do you have the living water? Are you greater than our father Jacob?' (verses 11f) indicates that she suspects that the words of the foreign Jewish rabbi hold a deeper secret which she wishes to understand. The response that Christ offers, 'the water that I shall give him will become in him a spring of water welling up as a source of life' (verse 14), implies a change in the level of meaning. It no longer refers to water that quenches thirst, nor to a 'living water' of the Torah. The water that Christ gives should become an independent living source within the human being. It is precisely this water that the woman seeks. She has a presentiment of something wonderful and new, as her entreaty shows. But her reply (verse 15) reveals that she has not fully grasped the ramifications of Christ's words. She expresses the hope that she need not come again to this well of Jacob to fetch water.

At this point, another change in the level of meaning occurs which seems like a jump in the text. Christ seems not to respond to her request for the water that becomes a source in humans, but rather tells her to 'call your husband.'

Here we may suspect a correlation between the 'living water' that Christ spoke of, and the 'husband', a correlation whose details must be clarified. What does the husband and the following five husbands have to do with this?

At this point, Origen may be of help once more. In his *Commentary on John,* one of the oldest extant commentaries of the New Testament, he interprets the five husbands of the woman as the five books of Moses.[8] Since the Samaritans acknowledged these five books of Moses to be the holy scriptural revelation of God, this would be an illuminating explanation. It would also clarify why Christ in no way judges the woman morally on account of her 'five husbands'.

Furthermore, the woman does not seem to perceive herself as a sinner. Rather, the words of Christ 'you have had five husbands' precipitates a new level of perception in her, that is, a recognition of his prophetic power. She says: 'Lord, I perceive that you, you are a prophet' (verse 19) with the repeated emphasis of 'you'. In Greek the pronoun is usually part of the verb and only rarely, as here, is the pronoun συ *(su,* you) added for emphasis.

Christ's words 'you have had five husbands' is all the more astonishing as he proceeds to say '... and he that you *now (νυν nun)* have *is not your husband.*' In Greek, the *nun* describes a moment of *kairos*, the particular, moment of grace, which needs to be seized. Could it be that in this moment, at this point of the dialogue, Christ wants to reveal himself as the 'husband' that she has not yet had? Is he the one, who according to the prophecies of the Old Testament will fulfil the Torah? Even when she says, 'I know that the Messiah is coming, he who is called the Christ.' (verse 25), she still cannot quite apprehend what she is saying. Nonetheless, she addresses him as a prophet. And this makes it possible in turn for Christ to make himself known to her with the words, 'I, I am' – the first of the self-revelations of Christ in the Gospel of John.[9]

With this revelation, a space opens up in the soul of the woman in which the familiar words of the Torah resound. Yahweh had also referred to himself as the 'I am, the I am' for example, in the burning bush.[10]

The self-revelation of Christ to the Samaritan woman is already prepared in the foregoing text of John's Gospel. John the Baptist intimates that Christ is the bridegroom' (John 3:29), an indication of a possible *unio mystica.*[11]

The level reached here in the text recalls to us Origen's rising or spiritual sense. Like him, one could see the nameless woman as a representation of the human soul. Since primal times the human soul has encountered Christ in a stream of spirituality through steady devoted religious practice. Through his direct dialogue with the soul Christ now awakens a hitherto unsuspected thirst that human beings have for the divine. He speaks of himself as a new 'gift' which can be recognised (verse 10), and from 'living water' that derives from him, which when acknowledged and accepted by human beings, can become a source of 'living water'.

In this context, we may more fully appreciate the statement made by Rudolf Steiner in summing up the conversation at the well: Christ is here the 'Herald of the independent self,' that is, the self that *recognises*, that *knows*.[12]

²⁶Οὐχὶ ταῦτα ἔδει παθεῖν τὸν Χριστὸν
καὶ εἰσελθεῖν εἰς τὴν δόξαν αὐτοῦ;
²⁷καὶ ἀρξάμενος ἀπὸ Μωϋσέως
καὶ ἀπὸ πάντων τῶν προφητῶν
διηρμήνευσεν αὐτοῖς ἐν πάσαις ταῖς γραφαῖς
τὰ περὶ ἑαυτοῦ.

אֵלִי אֵלִי לָמָה עֲזַבְתָּנִי

Passiontide

Did not the Christ have to suffer these things?

(Matt.27:26–54 and Psalm 22)

> [26] Did not the Christ have to suffer these things,
> so that he could enter into his glory?
> [27] And beginning with Moses
> he went through all the prophets
> and the scriptures, interpreting for them
> that which concerned himself.
> (Luke 24:26f)

These words were spoken by the Resurrected One himself, as initially unrecognised, he accompanies two of his disciples on the way to Emmaus. He led them to the insight that the suffering, death and resurrection of the Messiah in the Holy Scriptures were presaged realities given by the divine Word, but only became reality on earth through Christ. In the Tanakh, the Old Testament, there are many references to a Messiah (in Greek, *Christos*) which are taken up in the gospels and quoted, partly by Christ himself.[1] One of the seven words spoken (in the Aramaic dialect) from the cross is such a reference, originating from the first line of Psalm 22:

'My God, My God, why do you forsake me?'

All four evangelists describe the Passion and crucifixion of Christ. There are clear, occasionally even verbatim parallels in the descriptions, but there are also differences. Each of the four

²⁶Τότε ἀπέλυσεν αὐτοῖς τὸν Βαραββᾶν,
τὸν δὲ Ἰησοῦν φραγελλώσας
παρέδωκεν, ἵνα σταυρωθῇ.
²⁷Τότε οἱ στρατιῶται τοῦ ἡγεμόνος
παραλαβόντες τὸν Ἰησοῦν εἰς τὸ πραιτώριον
συνήγαγον ἐπ᾽ αὐτὸν ὅλην τὴν σπεῖραν·
²⁸καὶ ἐκδύσαντες αὐτὸν χλαμύδα κοκκίνην περιέθηκαν
   αὐτῷ
²⁹καὶ πλέξαντες στέφανον ἐξ ἀκανθῶν
ἐπέθηκαν ἐπὶ τῆς κεφαλῆς αὐτοῦ
καὶ κάλαμον ἐν τῇ δεξιᾷ αὐτοῦ,
καὶ γονυπετήσαντες ἔμπροσθεν αὐτοῦ, ἐνέπαιξαν αὐτῷ
   λέγοντες·
Χαῖρε, βασιλεῦ τῶν Ἰουδαίων,
³⁰καὶ ἐμπτύσαντες εἰς αὐτὸν
ἔλαβον τὸν κάλαμον, καὶ ἔτυπτον εἰς τὴν κεφαλὴν αὐτοῦ·
³¹καὶ ὅτε ἐνέπαιξαν αὐτῷ,
ἐξέδυσαν αὐτὸν τὴν χλαμύδα
καὶ ἐνέδυσαν αὐτὸν τὰ ἱμάτια αὐτοῦ,
καὶ ἀπήγαγον αὐτὸν εἰς τὸ σταυρῶσαι.
³²Ἐξερχόμενοι δὲ εὗρον ἄνθρωπον Κυρηναῖον,
ὀνόματι Σίμωνα·
τοῦτον ἠγγάρευσαν ἵνα ἄρῃ τὸν σταυρὸν αὐτοῦ.
³³Καὶ ἐλθόντες εἰς τόπον λεγόμενον Γολγοθᾶ,
ὅ ἐστιν, κρανίου τόπος, λεγόμενος,
³⁴ἔδωκαν αὐτῷ πιεῖν οἶνον μετὰ χολῆς μεμιγμένον·
καὶ γευσάμενος οὐκ ἠθέλησεν πιεῖν·

reports creates its own impressive picture of this event of Christ's Passion, an event that is almost impossible to comprehend. Although the evangelists lived at the time of the blossoming of ancient historical writing, it is quite obvious that neither the event, nor the style and method are appropriate to a historical description. gospels are proclamations, emissaries from the spiritual world. Part of Matthew's version of the Passion (27:26–54) provides us with the words from Psalm 22:

> [26]Then Pilate released to them Barabbas
> But Jesus he had scourged
> And handed him over, that he might be crucified
> [27]Then the soldiers of the governor took Jesus
> Led him into the praetorium
> And gathered around him the entire cohort of soldiers
> [28]And they stripped him, putting a scarlet robe around him
> [29]And they wove a crown of thorns
> Placing it on his head
> And gave him a reed-staff in his right hand,
> And falling on their knees before him, ridiculed him, shouting
> 'Hail to you, King of the Jews,'
> [30]And they spat at him,
> Took the reed-staff and beat him on the head,
> [31]And after they had ridiculed him,
> They took off the scarlet robe
> And dressed him in his clothes
> And led him forth to be crucified.
> [32]Going out, they came upon a man from Cyrene
> With the name, Simon
> They urgently pressed him into carrying his cross.
> [33]And as they came to the place called Golgotha
> Which means 'place of the skull'
> [34]They gave him wine to drink, mixed with gall
> And as he tasted it, he did not wish to drink

³⁵σταυρώσαντες δὲ αὐτὸν
διεμερίσαντο τὰ ἱμάτια αὐτοῦ, βάλλοντες κλῆρον,
³⁶καὶ καθήμενοι, ἐτήρουν αὐτὸν ἐκεῖ·
³⁷καὶ ἐπέθηκαν ἐπάνω τῆς κεφαλῆς αὐτοῦ
τὴν αἰτίαν αὐτοῦ γεγραμμένην·
ΟΥΤΟΣ ΕΣΤΙΝ ΙΕΣΟΥΣ,
Ο ΒΑΣΙΛΕΥΣ ΤΩΝ ΙΟΥΔΑΙΩΝ.
³⁸Τότε σταυροῦνται σὺν αὐτῷ δύο λησταί,
εἷς ἐκ δεξιῶν καὶ εἷς ἐξ εὐωνύμων.
³⁹Οἱ δὲ παραπορευόμενοι ἐβλασφήμουν αὐτὸν, κινοῦντες
    τὰς κεφαλὰς αυτῶν
⁴⁰καὶ λέγοντες· Ὁ καταλύων τὸν ναὸν
καὶ ἐν τρισὶν ἡμέραις οἰκοδομῶν,
σῶσον σεαυτόν εἰ Υἱὸς εἶ τοῦ Θεοῦ,
καὶ κατάβηθι ἀπὸ τοῦ σταυροῦ·
⁴¹ὁμοίως καὶ οἱ ἀρχιερεῖς ἐμπαίζοντες
μετὰ τῶν γραμματέων καὶ πρεσβυτέρων, ἔλεγον,
⁴²Ἄλλους ἔσωσες, ἑαυτὸν οὐ δύναται σῶσαι·
βασιλεὺς Ἰσραήλ ἐστιν,
καταβάτω νῦν ἀπὸ τοῦ σταυροῦ
καὶ πιστεύσομεν ἐπ᾽ αὐτόν·
⁴³πέποιθεν ἐπί τὸν Θεόν,
ῥυσάσθω νῦν εἰ θέλει αὐτόν·
εἶπεν γὰρ ὅτι Θεοῦ εἰμι Υἱός·
⁴⁴τὸ δ᾽αὐτὸ καὶ οἱ λησταὶ οἱ συσταυρωθέντες σὺν αὐτῷ,
    ὠνείδιζον αὐτόν.
⁴⁵Ἀπὸ δὲ ἕκτης ὥρας
σκότος ἐγένετο ἐπὶ πᾶσαν τὴν γῆν,
ἕως ὥρας ἐνάτης·
⁴⁶περὶ δὲ τὴν ἐνάτην ὥραν ἀνεβόησεν ὁ Ἰησοῦς φωνῇ
    μεγάλῃ λέγων·
Ἐλὶ, Ἐλὶ, λεμὰ σαβαχθάνι;
τοῦτ᾽ἔστιν· Θεέ μου, Θεέ μου, ἱνατί με ἐγκατέλιπες;
⁴⁷τινὲς δὲ τῶν ἐκεῖ ἑστηκότων, ἀκούσαντες, ἔλογον
ὅτι Ἠλίαν φωνεῖ οὗτος·

³⁵And when they had crucified him,
They divided his garments and cast lots
³⁶And sitting, they guarded him there,
³⁷And they placed above his head a writing
With his offence:
'THIS IS JESUS,
THE KING OF THE JEWS.'
³⁸There were crucified with him two thieves,
One to the right and one to the left.
³⁹Those who passed by, blasphemed, shaking their heads
⁴⁰And said, 'You will tear down the temple and build
    it up
In three days –
So save yourself, if you are God's Son!
Step down from the cross!'
⁴¹Likewise, the High Priests mocked
With the scribes and the elders, and said:
⁴²'He saved others, but he cannot save himself!
He is the King of Israel!
He should climb down from the cross,
Then we shall believe in him!
⁴³He has trusted in God,
Let him rescue him now – if he wants him!
For he had said: "I am the Son of God".'
⁴⁴The thieves also reproached him, those who were
    crucified with him.
⁴⁵From the sixth hour on
A darkness came over the land
Until the ninth hour.
⁴⁶In the ninth hour Jesus cried aloud:
'Eli, Eli, lema sabachtani.'
That means 'My God, my God, why do you forsake me?'
⁴⁷Several of those who were standing there, heard it and
    said:
'He is calling Elijah'

⁴⁸καὶ εὐθέως δραμὼν εἷς ἐξ αὐτῶν καὶ λαβὼν σπόγγον
πλήσας τε ὄξους καὶ περιθεὶς καλάμῳ
ἐπότιζεν αὐτόν·
⁴⁹οἱ δὲ λοιποὶ ἔλεγον· Ἄφες, ἴδωμεν
εἰ ἔρχεται Ἠλίας σώσων αὐτόν·
⁵⁰ὁ δὲ Ἰησοῦς πάλιν κράξας φωνῇ μεγάλῃ
ἀφῆκεν τὸ πνεῦμα.
⁵¹Καὶ ἰδοὺ
τὸ καταπέτασμα τοῦ ναοῦ
ἐσχίσθη
ἀπ' ἄνωθεν ἕως κάτω εἰς δύο,
καὶ ἡ γῆ ἐσείσθη, καὶ αἱ πέτραι ἐσχίσθησαν,
⁵²καὶ τὰ μνημεῖα ἀνεῴχθησαν
καὶ πολλὰ σώματα τῶν κεκοιμημένων ἁγίων
ἠγέρθησαν·
⁵³καὶ ἐξελθόντες ἐκ τῶν μνημείων μετὰ τὴν ἔγερσιν αὐτοῦ
εἰσῆλθον εἰς τὴν ἁγίαν πόλιν καὶ ἐνεφανίσθησαν πολλοῖς.
⁵⁴Ὁ δὲ ἑκατόνταρχος καὶ οἱ μετ' αὐτοῦ τηροῦντες τὸν Ἰησοῦν
ἰδόντες τὸν σεισμὸν καὶ τὰ γινόμενα
ἐφοβήθησαν σφόδρα, λέγοντες·
Ἀληθῶς
Θεοῦ Υἱὸς ἦν οὗτος.

¹אֵלִי אֵלִי לָמָה עֲזַבְתָּנִי
⁷כָּל־רֹאַי יַלְעִגוּ לִי יַפְטִירוּ בְשָׂפָה יָנִיעוּ רֹאשׁ:
⁸גֹּל אֶל־יְהוָה יְפַלְּטֵהוּ יַצִּילֵהוּ כִּי חָפֵץ בּוֹ:
¹⁵וּלְשׁוֹנִי מֻדְבָּק מַלְקוֹחָי
¹⁶הִקִּיפוּנִי כָּאֲרִי יָדַי וְרַגְלָי
¹⁸יְחַלְּקוּ בְגָדַי לָהֶם וְעַל־לְבוּשִׁי יַפִּילוּ גוֹרָל

⁴⁸And immediately, one of them came and having taken
   a sponge
Dipped it in sour wine, placed it on a stick
And gave it to him to drink.
⁴⁹The others said 'Leave it, we want to see
Whether Elijah will come and rescue him.'
⁵⁰Jesus cried again with a powerful voice
And gave up the spirit.
⁵¹And see –
The curtain of the Most Holy in the Temple
Was torn
From top to bottom, in two
And the earth quaked and the rocks were split
⁵²And the tombs opened,
And the bodies of many holy ones, having fallen asleep
Were awakened,
⁵³And they came – after his resurrection –
Out of the tombs, and appeared to many
⁵⁴As the centurion and those with him guarding Jesus
Saw the earthquake, and that what happened,
They became filled with great fear and spoke:
'Truly –
This was and is the Son of God!'

It is striking, how many passages from this text echo almost verbatim the Twenty-Second Psalm. They appear to be as a conversation between the two texts:
Verse 1: My God, my God, who do you forsake me?
Verse 7: All who see me mock me, they make mouths at me,
   they shake their heads.
Verse 8: He called to God – he should deliver him, should
   rescue him, if he delights in him.
Verse 15: my tongue cleaves to my jaws
Verse 16: they have pierced my hands and feet...
Verse 18: they divide my garments between them, and they
   cast lots for my cloak.

In contemplating the two texts, the similarities between the Psalm of David and the representation of the Passion are unmistakable. The proposal that Matthew had simply 'copied' out of the Psalm does not do the theme justice, and does not satisfy as an explanation. But what is happening here? Is it conceivable that there is a connection between *prophesied* reality and, centuries later, *lived* reality on the earth? Such a connection was implied to the two disciples on the way to Emmaus by the unrecognised Christ: 'And beginning with Moses he went through all the scriptures and the prophets, interpreting for them that which concerned himself.' (Luke 24:27).

With the abundance of quoted references from the Old Testament in the whole of the New Testament, Christ's and his disciples' self-evident and active living with the Scriptures is amply documented. Could it be that in his version of the Passion of Christ, Matthew is led to a dawning comprehension of the immensity of this event through the familiar praying and singing of this Psalm?[2]

In this account, it is above all the words of Christ from the cross, 'My God, my God, why do you forsake me?' that have moved hearts over the centuries, and have prompted composers like Heinrich Schütz, Haydn, Gubaidulina to put these words to music. The words are from Christ in the deepest moment of his being human, deserted and in the solitariness of death; from the suffering God, who can empathise with and come closer to suffering human beings.

Reading the Psalm to the end, we find an astonishing shift. From the last word in verse 21 עניתני *('anitani)* 'you answer me', without any apparent transition, the Psalm becomes a tremendous celebratory hymn.

An 'answer' to the psalmist, which is not recorded in words, effects the transformation of the bitter dirge which flinches in the face of death, to one complete song of praise. The transformation is expressed in the most noteworthy verses:

²²I will tell of your name to my brethren; in the midst of the congregation I will praise you ...
²³You who honour the I-AM, praise him, all you sons of Jacob, glorify him ...
²⁶... those who seek the I-AM shall praise him, their heart will remain living forever ...
³¹... they shall come and proclaim your truth to a people, who are yet to be born, that he has fulfilled it.

What has happened? At the nadir of destitution, solitude, and doubt, the psalmist palpably experiences the other side of the reality of death, which initiates a transformation in him.

We can find a parallel to this turning point in the Psalm in Matthew's account of the Passion – in the words of the Roman centurion and his companions: 'truly, this *was and is* the son of God' (verse 54). The grammatical form of the verb which is in the original Greek text is ἦν *(ēn)*, an imperfect. It does not express a past form – 'this *has been* God's son' – but rather, indicates a deed that is not yet finished. Could there be in this phrasing of the uncompleted deed, a deed which is yet open and further-reaching, a hint of the glory of the resurrection which is yet to pass? 'Truly – this *was and is* the Son of God!'

Matthew writes retrospectively in full awareness of the event of the resurrection. This consciousness is immutably present for him. And as such it is also included in the rejoicing transition of the Psalm.

In the light of Psalm 22 and the text from Matthew, Steiner's general exposition can also be read anew. His formulation for these words sound contradictory, 'My God, my God, how you have glorified me.'³ This is not a different, or perhaps even correct translation of the passage, as is sometimes claimed by anthroposophists. In this translation, the fact of the earthly suffering and the agony of the death of Jesus Christ on the cross are not negated. Rather, Steiner points to the mystery-nature of the Passion event. The experience undergone in the mysteries by the neophyte of a symbolic death and resurrection are fulfilled by

Christ as historical fact.[4] What Steiner describes in the strange and unusual rendering 'how you have glorified me,' instead of 'why have you forsaken me?' is the view from the other side of the very same process. These words mirror the transition to joy in Psalm 22.

In some medieval representations, the crucified one already has the gesture of the resurrection as if *impressed within* him. The attendant human figure attempts to grasp this with his hands or to listen and understand it at the heart of Christ.

PASSIONTIDE

Deposition from the cross, chapel portal, Tirol Castle, around 1170 (Wikimedia-ManfredK)

¹¹Μαρία δὲ εἱστήκει πρὸς τῷ μνημείῳ ἔξω κλαίουσα·
ὡς οὖν ἔκλαιεν, παρέκυψεν εἰς τὸ μνημεῖον,
¹²καὶ θεωρεῖ δύο ἀγγέλους
ἐν λευκοῖς καθεζομένους,
ἕνα πρὸς τῇ κεφαλῇ καὶ ἕνα πρὸς τοῖς ποσίν,
ὅπου ἔκειτο τὸ σῶμα τοῦ Ἰησοῦ·
¹³καὶ λέγουσιν αὐτῇ ἐκεῖνοι· Γύναι, τί κλαίεις;
λέγει αὐτοῖς ὅτι ἦραν τὸν Κύριόν μου,
καὶ οὐκ οἶδα ποῦ ἔθηκαν αὐτόν·
¹⁴ταῦτα εἰποῦσα,
ἐστράφη εἰς τὰ ὀπίσω,
καὶ θεωρεῖ τὸν Ἰησοῦν ἑστῶτα,
καὶ οὐκ ᾔδει ὅτι Ἰησοῦς ἐστιν·
¹⁵λέγει αὐτῇ Ἰησοῦς·
Γύναι, τί κλαίεις; τίνα ζητεῖς;
ἐκείνη δοκοῦσα ὅτι ὁ κηπουρός ἐστιν, λέγει αὐτῷ·
Κύριε, εἰ σὺ ἐβάστασας αὐτόν,
εἰπέ μοι ποῦ ἔθηκας αὐτόν,
κἀγὼ αὐτὸν ἀρῶ·
¹⁶λέγει αὐτῇ Ἰησοῦς·
Μαριάμ·
στραφεῖσα ἐκείνη λέγει αὐτῷ Ἑβραϊστί,
Ῥαββουνί, (ὃ λέγεται, Διδάσκαλε)·
¹⁷λέγει αὐτῇ Ἰησοῦς·
Μή μου ἅπτου,
οὔπω γὰρ ἀναβέβηκα πρὸς τὸν Πατέρα·

Easter Sunday

Mary of Magdala and the twice-turning

(John 20:11–18)

¹¹Now Mary stood outside at the tomb, weeping –
Whilst weeping, she stooped down into the tomb
¹²And sees two angels sitting
In light shining
One at the head, one at the feet
Where they had laid the body of Jesus
¹³And these spoke to her, 'Woman, why do you weep?'
She said to them, 'They have taken away my Lord,
And I do not know where they have laid him.'
¹⁴As she says this
She is turned, backwards
And sees Jesus, standing,
And does not know that it is Jesus
¹⁵Jesus says to her,
'Woman, why do you weep? Whom do you seek?'
She, thinking that he was the gardener, says to him,
'Lord, if you have taken him away,
Tell me, where have you laid him?
I want to take him back.'
¹⁶Jesus says to her,
'Mary,'
Once more turning, she says,
'Rabbuni' (that means 'my master')
¹⁷Jesus says to her,
'Do not touch me,
As I am not yet ascended to my Father.

> πορεύου δὲ πρὸς τοὺς ἀδελφούς μου καὶ εἰπὲ αὐτοῖς·
> Ἀναβαίνω πρὸς τὸν Πατέρα μου καὶ Πατέρα ὑμῶν
> καὶ Θεόν μου καὶ Θεὸν ὑμῶν·
> [18]ἔρχεται Μαριὰμ ἡ Μαγδαληνὴ ἀγγέλλουσα τοῖς μαθηταῖς
> ὅτι ἑώρακα τὸν κύριον,
> καὶ ταῦτα εἶπεν αὐτῇ.

> But go to my brothers and tell them:
> I am going up to my Father and to your Father,
> To my God and to your God.'
> ¹⁸Mary of Magdala comes and tells the disciples,
> 'I have seen the Lord and
> These things he has said to me.'

Mary of Magdala

Who was Mary of Magdala, usually referred to as Mary Magdalene? No other figure of the New Testament from the successors of Jesus Christ has so occupied people's hearts and minds as she has. One assumes that her name emanates from her home, the small town of Magdala, today Migdal by the Sea of Galilee. All four evangelists repeatedly refer to her, as well as several of Apocryphal documents.[1] Such a figure has naturally been a great source of material for fiction.[2] On top of this, there is a whole range of artwork exploring this character, from Carolingian times right through to the twentieth century.[3]

From the many stories handed down concerning her, the focus in word or image has concentrated on differing aspects. It is either on the transformation effected in her by the exorcism of her seven 'demons' (Luke 8:2 and Mark 16:9). Or it is devoted to the anointing on the eve of the Passion of Jesus of Nazareth. With the most precious of oils – spikenard (or nard) that was an integral part of the death rituals – she anoints him and thereby confers the name Χριστος, Christ – that is, the anointed one – upon him. Or she appears kneeling or standing under the cross with the disciple John and the mother of Jesus (Matt.27:55f). Or her encounter with the Risen One is depicted in the garden on Easter Sunday morning (Mark 16:9–11, Matt.28:9–10, John 20:14–18) where *noli me tangere* is the theme.

The manner in which Mary was perceived also changed over the centuries. Afforded great respect by some, for example Hippolytus of Rome (170–235), the Church Father who in his

Apostola Apostolorum called her the 'apostle of apostles', she has also been labelled a sinner or even prostitute, from which the institution of Magdalene asylums for 'fallen women' derived its name.

A particular difficulty concerning Mary is the lack of clarity as to *who she is* in the gospels. The Catholic Church differentiates between Mary of Magdala and Mary of Bethany, the sister of Lazarus, the woman who anoints Christ. The Protestant Church even recognises three Marys: an unknown sinner from the story of the anointing according to Luke (7:36–50) as well as Mary of Bethany (Luke 10:38–42) and Mary of Magdala.

It is just this fluctuating complex atmosphere of mystery surrounding Mary that lends her an aura which has always attracted people of the most varied cultures and times. If we immerse ourselves in the insoluble question as to whether she is a single or composite figure, whether there is some historical person behind this figure, or if we simply allow the essence of the many traditional legends to work on us, then it is clear that we are concerned with an extraordinary and strong personality.

An illuminating subtext for the encounter of Mary of Magdala with the Risen One, seems to me to be the story of the anointing in Bethany (John 12:1–8; Mark 14:3–9; Matt.26:6–13; Luke 7:36–50).

All four gospels report – each with only slight variation – the following. At a repast in Bethany, in the house of Simon the leper, to which Christ and his followers are invited and were at table, a woman enters (only in John is she named as Mary) and breaks the sealed lid of an alabaster jar, in which precious nard oil is stored. She pours this oil on the head of Jesus. According to Luke and John, she weeps prostrate at his feet, kissing them, anointing them with the nard oil and drying them with her long hair. The fragrance carries through the house. The disciples become indignant over this incomprehensible waste. In just a few minutes, an oil worth the equivalent to a whole year's wage (300 denarii) is poured out. The woman utters no sound, but simply acts. Jesus who, through her deed, becomes 'the anointed one' –

the literal meaning of *Christ* – speaks for her and her action: 'She has put the oil on my body, for my burial. Amen, I say to you that wherever in the world *this* gospel is preached, in her memory it shall be related what she has done.' (Matt.26:12f).

With these words, Christ attests to the high level of appreciation for the person of Mary of Magdala. Her unusual deed, which was so heavily disapproved of by those around her, thereby acquired a sacrosanct character. Christ does not speak here in general of a later promulgation of a gospel, but rather the proclamation in the whole world of '*this* gospel'. He indicates that it is this gospel, 'these good tidings' of his death and resurrection, which has begun with this deed of anointing before death.

Out of the various reports in the New Testament, a picture of a woman emerges who is capable of wise foresight, of grand extravagance and also of an act of selfless, devoted love.

The twofold turning

On Easter morning Mary of Magdala appears in deep mourning, weeping when she finds the tomb empty. If we follow the course of the narrative, we may discern a development. It leads through various levels of perception and encounter to a recognition of the Resurrected Christ – like an *awakening* to a different degree of consciousness.

Already at the beginning of the narrative, Mary of Magdala has a degree of spiritual-soul vision; through her tears, she can perceive the angels inside the tomb 'in light shining' (verse 12) and can hear their question concerning the reason for her tears.

During the process of answering ('They have taken away my Lord and I do not know where they have laid him,' verse 13), something happens to her. She is turned, toward the area behind her back (verse 14). This back-ground is often portrayed in painting and even in the scenery of theatre backdrops as the spiritual sphere of inspiration.

At this point, the grammatical form of the verb στρεφω *(strephō)* is apposite.[4] It is in the aorist passive, that is, the boundless, timeless tense, and the passive expresses what is being done to or with Mary. Out of this inner dynamic she perceives anew, seeing the Risen One, the Christ whom she takes to be the gardener. As the Resurrected One is not in a material form, it is clear that Mary is clairaudient – she has the ability to hear something physically inaudible – in that she understands the question put to her. But she has not yet recognised him; rather she sees in him someone expected and fitting in the surroundings of a garden, the gardener.[5] She requests him to return the body of her lord (verse 15).

However, in the moment where she is spoken to by the Risen One by her name, 'Mary', she is turned *(στραφεισα, strapheisa)* about once more.[6] The grammatical form expresses it concisely: she finds herself *within* a process (the form expressed by the participle). It is not *she* who is active, but rather she is passively moved by something greater than her. But now there is something remarkable, for this second turning about is, from a purely physical point of view, nonsensical as she had only just turned toward Christ. The text is thus implying that this turning is not an external one, but rather an inner process on a quite different level, one that awakens her to the new illuminating recognition: 'Rabbuni,' my master (verse 16).

Noli me tangere

To this tenderly spoken 'Rabbuni' (so often been the subject of portrayal in paintings which have sought to capture the devotion and inner loving gesture of Mary toward Christ) the reply comes 'do not touch me' (verse 17), which in Latin is the well-known phrase *noli me tangere*. It is quite certain that this should not be interpreted (as it occasionally is, in accord with the concomitant negative image of Mary of Magdala) as 'do not touch me, you impure woman!' That would clearly contradict everything said about her by Christ. Rather, it is implied that the body of the newly Risen One, a non physical-material body, cannot yet be touched by profane human hands.

EASTER SUNDAY

If we recall the quite disparate invitation to the disciple Thomas, that Christ makes just a few verses later (John 20:27), 'reach your finger here and look on my hands, and bring your hand and put it into my side.' then we seem to be faced with a contradiction. If the text is precisely followed, however, it disappears. Following Christ's words of invitation, there is no indication that Thomas actually did this. It is only through the endless famous paintings of this moment that the common perception is that Thomas actually obtained his proof. Yet in the gospel, there is no mention of this. Merely the words of the invitation of Christ to feel his wounds is enough to precipitate the recognition, and Thomas confesses, 'My Lord and my God!' The answer is thereupon given by Christ: 'because you have *beheld* me, you have believed. Blessed are the *non-seeing* and yet believing.'[7]

It is striking that there are two verbs used by Christ for 'seeing', and therefore two different qualities are implied. This could lead us to revise our usual interpretation of Christ's words as an exhortation to blindly believe. Indeed, Christ merely confirms in the first sentence the discerning vision of Thomas which he had expressed in his confession. In the second sentence, he describes another form of seeing, that of the believer, who is at peace, who is blessed, without having to behold.[8] One can read both these sentences, without any implied intimation of admonition on Christ's part. Rather, it can be read as a description of differing conditions and capacities of spiritual development.

Mary of Magdala and the disciple Thomas are two quite different people of different spiritual abilities. Their meetings with the Risen One were disparate in character but contain only apparent contradictions. Rudolf Steiner articulated it in the following manner: 'The women and the disciples saw Christ in the ether body, no longer Jesus of Nazareth but the Christ, the transformed inner human being.'[9]

> The Evangelists wish particularly to evoke the impression that the Christ appeared in this altered form [after the burial]. But they also wish to indicate something else.

> *For the Christ to exert influence on human soul, a certain receptivity in those souls was necessary* ... What the Christ brought about from person to person after the so-called Resurrection was something that worked up from the unconscious soul-powers of the disciples into their soul-life: an acquaintance with the Son. *Hence the differences in the portrayal of the Risen Christ; hence, too, the variations in the accounts, showing how the Christ appeared to one or other person,* according to the disposition of the person concerned. Here we see the Christ-Being acting on the subconscious part of the souls of the disciples; hence the appearances are quite individual, and we should not complain because they are not uniform.[10]

Mary from Magdala is the first person whom the Risen One encounters, and she is the only one whom he meets alone. All other encounters, including the one with Thomas, occur in a group.

She is given the task by Christ to proclaim the gospel of death and resurrection to the disciples, from where it spread out over the world.

α
και μ[
εμου[
πηρ ε[
αυτω[
πηρ ο[
ιησου[
τ̣ουτ[
εις εμε[
τον π[ρ
λειτε τ[
ματα ε[

¹³Καὶ ἰδοὺ
δύο ἐξ αὐτῶν ἐν αὐτῇ τῇ ἡμέρᾳ
ἦσαν πορευόμενοι εἰς κώμην
ἀπέχουσαν σταδίους ἑξήκοντα ἀπὸ Ἱερουσαλήμ,
ᾗ ὄνομα Ἐμμαοῦς,
¹⁴καὶ αὐτοὶ ὡμίλουν πρὸς ἀλλήλους
περὶ πάντων τῶν συμβεβηκότων τούτων·
¹⁵καὶ ἐγένετο
ἐν τῷ ὁμιλεῖν αὐτοὺς
καὶ συζητεῖν,
καὶ αὐτὸς Ἰησοῦς ἐγγίσας συνεπορεύετο αὐτοῖς·
¹⁶οἱ δὲ ὀφθαλμοὶ αὐτῶν ἐκρατοῦντο
τοῦ μὴ ἐπιγνῶναι αὐτόν·
¹⁷εἶπεν δὲ πρὸς αὐτούς·
Τίνες οἱ λόγοι οὗτοι οὓς ἀντιβάλλετε
πρὸς ἀλλήλους περιπατοῦντες;
καὶ ἐστάθησαν, σκυθρωποί·
¹⁸ἀποκριθεὶς δὲ εἷς ὀνόματι Κλεοπᾶς
εἶπεν πρὸς αὐτόν·
Σὺ μόνος παροικεῖς Ἰηρουσαλὴμ
καὶ οὐκ ἔγνως τὰ
γενόμενα ἐν αὐτῇ ἐν ταῖς ἡμέραις ταύταις;
¹⁹καὶ εἶπεν αὐτοῖς·
Ποῖα;

Eastertime

Were not our hearts burning within us?

The way to Emmaus (Luke 24:13–32)

¹³And see,
Two of them were journeying on this day,
On the way to a village,
Sixty stadia away from Jerusalem,
Emmaus by name.
¹⁴And they conversed with *one another, together*
About everything that had happened.
¹⁵And it happened, that
In this their togetherness and
In their *mutual questing search*
Jesus himself approached and took up the path with them
¹⁶But their eyes were held by a force.
They did not recognise him.
¹⁷And he spoke to them,
'Which words are you moving back and forth
Whilst you walk with each other?'
Then they stood still, looking sadly.
¹⁸One of them, Cleopas his name, replied
And spoke to him,
'Are you the only one, you, a stranger in Jerusalem,
Who does not know the events
Which have occurred there in these days?'
¹⁹And he spoke to them,
'Which?'

οἱ δὲ εἶπεν αὐτῷ·
Τὰ περὶ Ἰησοῦ τοῦ Ναζαρηνοῦ,
ὃς ἐγένετο ἀνὴρ προφήτης
δυνατὸς ἐν ἔργῳ καὶ λόγῳ
ἐναντίον τοῦ θεοῦ καὶ παντὸς τοῦ λαοῦ,
[20]ὅπως τε παρέδωκαν αὐτὸν οἱ ἀρχιερεῖς
καὶ οἱ ἄρχοντες ἡμῶν
εἰς κρίμα θανάτου
καὶ ἐσταύρωσαν αὐτόν·
[21]ἡμεῖς δὲ ἠλπίζομεν ὅτι αὐτός ἐστιν
ὁ μέλλων λυτροῦσθαι τὸν Ἰσραήλ·
ἀλλά γε καὶ σὺν πᾶσιν τούτοις
τρίτην ταύτην ἡμέραν ἄγει
ἀφ' οὗ ταῦτα ἐγένετο·
[22]ἀλλὰ καὶ γυναῖκές τινες ἐξ ἡμῶν
ἐξέστησαν ἡμᾶς,
γενόμεναι ὀρθριναὶ ἐπὶ τὸ μνημεῖον,
[23]καὶ μὴ εὑροῦσαι τὸ σῶμα αὐτοῦ
ἦλθον λέγουσαι καὶ ὀπτασίαν ἀγγέλων ἑωρακέναι,
οἵ λέγουσιν
αὐτὸν ζῆν·
[24]καὶ ἀπῆλθόν τινες τῶν σὺν ἡμῖν ἐπὶ τὸ μνημεῖον,
καὶ εὗρον οὕτως καθὼς καὶ αἱ γυναῖκες εἶπον,
αὐτὸν δὲ οὐκ εἶδον·
[25]καὶ αὐτὸς εἶπεν πρὸς αὐτούς·
Ὦ ἀνόητοι
καὶ βραδεῖς τῇ καρδίᾳ
τοῦ πιστεύειν ἐπὶ πᾶσιν
οἷς ἐλάλησαν οἱ προφῆται·
[26]οὐχὶ ταῦτα ἔδει παθεῖν τὸν Χριστὸν
καὶ εἰσελθεῖν εἰς τὴν δόξαν αὐτοῦ;
[27]καὶ ἀρξάμενος
ἀπὸ Μωϋσέως καὶ ἀπὸ πάντων τῶν προφητῶν
διηρμήνευσεν αὐτοῖς ἐν πάσαις ταῖς γραφαῖς
τὰ περὶ ἑαυτοῦ.

They said now to him,
'Those of Jesus, the Nazarene,
Who was a man, who bore the divine in his speech,
Immensely powerful in word and deed
In the face of God and before all the people.
[20]And this is why our high priests
And elders
Handed him over to be condemned to death –
And they crucified him.
[21]We, however, carried the hope that he was chosen
To redeem Israel.
And after all of this,
Today is the third day
Since this happened.
[22]Some of our women have also
Confounded us,
Those who were at the tomb at dawn
[23]They found no body and came and said,
That they had seen the face of the angels,
And they had said:
He lives.
[24]And several of us went together then to the tomb
And found it just as the women had said.
But him they found not.'
[25]And he spoke to them:
'O you who are without *heart-understanding,*
Who are *slow of heart*
Who do not trust in all that
Which has been said by God-speaking-men.
[26]Did not the Christ have to suffer all of this,
So that he might enter into his glory?'
[27]And he began to through-interpret
From Moses and all the prophets
And all the Scriptures,
Which spoke of him.

²⁸Καὶ ἤγγισαν εἰς τὴν κώμην οὗ ἐπορούοντο,
καὶ αὐτὸς προσεποιήσατο πορρώτερον πορεύεσθαι·
²⁹καὶ παρεβιάσαντο αὐτὸν λέγοντες·
Μεῖνον μεθ' ἡμῶν,
ὅτι πρὸς ἑσπέραν ἐστὶν
καὶ κέκλικεν ἤδη ἡ ἡμέρα·
καὶ εἰσῆλθεν
τοῦ μεῖναι σὺν αὐτοῖς·
³⁰καὶ ἐγένετο
ἐν τῷ κατακλιθῆναι αὐτὸν μετ' αὐτῶν,
λαβὼν τὸν ἄρτον
εὐλόγησεν
καὶ κλάσας, ἐπεδίδου αὐτοῖς·
³¹αὐτῶν δὲ διηνοίχθησαν οἱ ὀφθαλμοί,
καὶ ἐπέγνωσαν αὐτόν·
καὶ αὐτὸς ἄφαντος ἐγένετο ἀπ' αὐτῶν.
³²Καὶ εἶπαν πρὸς ἀλλήλους·
Οὐχὶ ἡ καρδία ἡμῶν καιομένη ἦν ἐν ἡμῖν,
ὡς ἐλάλει ἡμῖν ἐν τῇ ὁδῷ,
ὡς διήνοιγεν ἡμῖν τὰς γραφάς;

> ²⁸And it happened, that they came to the village
> And he *made as if to go on further,*
> ²⁹They implored him, however, and spoke,
> 'Abide with us,
> For evening is nearing,
> And the day is drawing to a close.'
> And he went inside with them,
> To abide with them and to dwell.
> ³⁰And there it happened,
> As he reclined to eat with them,
> That he took the bread,
> And blessed,
> Broke it, and gave it to them,
> ³¹That their eyes were *opened-through*
> And they recognised him.
> But he disappeared from them.
> ³²And they spoke to one another:
> 'Were not our hearts burning within us,
> As he spoke with us on the way,
> As he opened-throughout the Scriptures to us?'

All the descriptions of human experience of the Risen One are united in their view that recognition of the Christ does not happen with immediate clarity, but reveals itself in steps. In this fashion, Mary Magdalene perceives Christ first as the gardener. Only when her name is spoken by him, are her 'eyes opened' to reality. The disciple Thomas, similarly, gains his certainty only after experiencing profound doubt.

It is said of the two disciples who were walking to Emmaus, that something like a force hindering recognition held them in thrall (verse 16). This force of non-recognising remains effective throughout their entire journey. Not the conversations in which they attempt to comprehend the recent events, nor the explanations of the Scriptures by Christ himself, nor his elucidation of the suffering, death and resurrection of the Son of God, leads them to recognition. The two disciples' experience of the Risen One develops through different levels.

We can follow a trace of the different levels of experience that they passed through if we examine the italicised parts of the text. Their way leads to cognition in another dimension – a perceiving of Christ in the etheric, as this experience is termed by Rudolf Steiner. The text describes this vividly when it says in verse 31 that 'their eyes were opened-through and they recognised him.'

The name of the village of their destination, Emmaus, means 'warming spring' and may recall the words of Christ to the woman of Samaria at the well, when he says there that 'a spring of water welling up as a source of life' must arise in the individual (John 4:14). It is also fitting that in the name of the disciples' destination, the 'warming spring', we find an echo in their recognition of Christ, 'Were not our hearts burning within us?' (verse 32).

To be able to perceive the Risen One those who see him are usually in a group with others.[1] In our text this mutual accord is emphasised by a conspicuous tautological form, which appears at first glance to be quite unnecessary. And so we find that the two conversed 'with one another, together' (verse 14), and that in their 'mutual questing search' (verse 15), the stranger appeared.

A further precondition for the perceiving in the etheric seems to be that the heart must be opened as an organ of cognition. In two ways Christ expresses this to the disciples when, through the pronounced exclamation, He points out that they are 'without heart-understanding,' and that they are 'slow of heart' (verse 25). An opening of their hearts is carefully prepared here, even if the disciples have not yet realised it, and it only becomes clear to them on looking back over their experience. Christ 'interprets' for them the writings of the prophets and of Moses, and what they have said of him. The Greek word for interpret, $διηρμνευσεν$ *(di(h)ērmēneusen)* contains the name of the messenger-god, 'Hermes' and indicates thereby that cognition always requires that two principle dimensions, 'the heavens and the earth', must come together. Only then can it become fruitful. In this as well, the Greek text is particularly descriptive. It places the prefix 'through' in front of the verb 'to interpret', something that is difficult to express in a modern European language. This prefix δια *(dia)*, through(out), appears three times in the text at key points in the path of recognition: He began to '*through*-interpret' to them the Holy Scriptures (verse 27), 'their eyes were opened-*through*' (verse 31) and at the end of the text, when the disciples in retrospective understanding of their experience of the Risen One, formulate it thus: 'Were not our hearts burning within us ... as he opened-*throughout* the Scriptures to us?' (verse 32).[2]

An important and at first somewhat puzzling point of the path of recognition is, 'he made as if to go on further' (verse 28). Instinctively we ask ourselves whether and why Christ professes to have something else to do. Is it a mistake? Rudolf Frieling points out that there is another episode in the gospels in which Christ apparently means to go on, to pass by: during the walking on the water (Mark 6:48).[3] Taking this into consideration, it becomes apparent that the disciples are being challenged to supply some form of their own initiative and forces of will to this initial gift of grace, the appearance of the Risen One. Christ's entering into the inner (the 'ship' in Mark 6:51) or, as in this particular text, 'he went inside' (verse 29) – that is, into the house, into the inner being of man. This does not happen automatically. To receive, hold and to lead within, a gift of the Spirit requires a degree of will and humility. This is indicated in the Greek word παρεβιασαντο *(parebiasanto)* 'they implored him' that is, with strength of will. This clear, willed imploring activity of the two disciples is imperative for them to recognise him in the gesture which similarly unfolds in stages (verse 30):

> That he took the bread,
> And blessed,
> Broke it, and gave it to them,

Only now, after completing the various stages of their way, and through their searching conversation, can the recognition become a reality. This happens only for a brief moment of fulfilment. For immediately after this, the text makes clear that Christ disappeared from their sight (verse 31). If we look at this text with Origen's moral sense, that is, with the question, what does this say to my soul, then the word παρουσια *(parousia)* may occur to us, a word often confused in translation with the concept of the second coming of Christ. The story of the experience of the Resurrected One, presented in this text as a path of ascending levels of cognition, can be understood as an experience of the Parousia of Christ in the original Greek sense of the word of presence, proximity, ubiquity and companionship. It becomes clear to us then that Parousia refers to the present moment and not to a 'return' in an indefinite future.

Since the death and resurrection of Christ on Golgotha, we live in this 'presence and companionship' of the Christ. To be able to recognise this at given moments requires spiritual effort and grace.

α
και μ
εμου
πηρ ε
αυτω
πηρ σ
ιησου
ρ ουτ
εις με
τον π
λει τε
ματα ε

Τὸν μὲν πρῶτον λόγον ἐποιησάμην περὶ πάντων,
ὦ Θεόφιλε,
ὧν ἤρξατο ὁ Ἰησοῦς ποιεῖν τε καὶ διδάσκειν,
²ἄχρι ἧς ἡμέρας
ἐντειλάμενος τοῖς ἀποστόλοις
διὰ Πνεύματος Ἁγίου οὓς ἐξελέξατο, ἀνελήμφθη·
³οἷς καὶ παρέστησεν ἑαυτὸν ζῶντα
μετὰ τὸ παθεῖν αὐτὸν,
ἐν πολλοῖς τεκμηρίοις,
δι' ἡμερῶν τεσσεράκοντα ὀπτανόμενος αὐτοῖς
καὶ λέγων τὰ περὶ τῆς βασιλείας τοῦ Θεοῦ·
⁴καὶ συναλιζόμενος
παρήγγειλεν αὐτοῖς
ἀπὸ Ἱεροσολύμων μὴ χωρίζεσθαι,
ἀλλὰ περιμένειν τὴν ἐπαγγελίαν τοῦ Πατρὸς
ἣν ἠκούσατέ μου·
⁵ὅτι Ἰωάννης μὲν ἐβάπτισεν ὕδατι,
ὑμεῖς δὲ ἐν Πνεύματι βαπτισθήσεσθε Ἁγίῳ,
οὐ μετὰ πολλὰς ταύτας ἡμέρας.
⁶Οἱ μὲν οὖν συνελθόντες
ἠρώτων αὐτὸν, λέγοντες·
Κύριε, εἰ ἐν τῷ χρόνῳ τούτῳ ἀποκαθιστάνεις
τὴν βασιλείαν τῷ Ἰσραήλ;

Ascension

Why do you stand looking into the heavens?

The disciples experience Ascension (Acts 1:1–12)

In the first book, I have brought everything to word,
O Friend of God,
Which Jesus had begun to do and to teach –
²Until the day, when he was received up –
Giving aim to the apostles,
Whom he had chosen through the Holy Spirit.
³To these he showed himself as the living
After his sufferings.
In many signs,
Through forty days he let himself be *perceived* by them
While he *spoke of 'that' about the Kingdom of God.*
⁴And while they *held the meal with one another*
He directed them
Not to leave Jerusalem
But to wait for the promise of the Father:
'Of which you have heard through me;
⁵Since John baptised with water,
But you are to be baptised into the Holy Spirit
Not long after these days.'
⁶They who were now *gathered together*
Asked him and *spoke*:
'Kyrie, will you restore again in this time
The kingdom for Israel?'

⁷εἶπεν δὲ πρὸς αὐτούς·
Οὐχ ὑμῶν ἐστιν γνῶναι χρόνους ἢ καιροὺς
οὓς ὁ Πατὴρ ἔθετο ἐν τῇ ἰδίᾳ ἐξουσίᾳ,
⁸ἀλλὰ λήμψεσθε δύναμιν
ἐπελθόντος τοῦ Ἁγίου Πνεύματος ἐφ᾽ ὑμᾶς,
καὶ ἔσεσθέ μου μάρτυρες ἔν τε Ἱερουσαλὴμ
καὶ ἐν πάσῃ τῇ Ἰουδαίᾳ καὶ Σαμαρείᾳ καὶ ἕως ἐσχάτου
   τῆς γῆς·
⁹καὶ ταῦτα εἰπὼν βλεπόντων αὐτῶν
ἐπήρθη,
καὶ νεφέλη ὑπέλαβεν αὐτὸν ἀπὸ τῶν ὀφθαλμῶν αὐτῶν·
¹⁰καὶ ὡς ἀτενίζοντες ἦσαν
εἰς τὸν οὐρανὸν
πορευομένου αὐτοῦ, καὶ ἰδοὺ
ἄνδρες δύο παρειστήκεισαν αὐτοῖς
ἐν ἐσθήσεσι λευκαῖς,
¹¹οἵ καὶ εἶπαν· Ἄνδρες Γαλιλαῖοι, τί ἑστήκατε
βλέποντες εἰς τὸν οὐρανόν;
οὗτος ὁ Ἰησοῦς ὁ ἀναλημφθεὶς
ἀφ᾽ ὑμῶν εἰς τὸν οὐρανὸν οὕτως
ἐλεύσεται ὃν τρόπον ἐθεάσασθε αὐτὸν
πορευόμενον εἰς τὸν οὐρανόν.
¹²Τότε ὑπέστρεψαν εἰς Ἱερουσαλὴμ ἀπὸ ὄρους
τοῦ καλουμένου Ἐλαιῶνος,
ὅ ἐστιν ἐγγὺς Ἱερουσαλὴμ σαββάτου ἔχον ὁδόν.

ASCENSION

> ⁷But he answered them:
> 'It is not given to you to know times and moments,
> Which the Father in his own *exousia* has set,
> ⁸But you will receive a power
> When the Holy Spirit descends upon you,
> And you will be my heralds in Jerusalem
> And all of Judea and Samaria, even to the end of the earth.'
> ⁹And as he *spoke* this, they were *perceiving*
> That he was being raised up
> And a cloud took him on high, out of their eyes.
> ¹⁰And while they were steadfast
> In their *seeing* in the heavens,
> He *changed*, and see,
> Two men came forth to them,
> In gleaming apparel, full of light,
> ¹¹And they said: 'You men of Galilee, why do you stand
> *Looking* into the heavens?
> This Jesus, who has been received up
> Away from you into the heavens,
> Will come in the same way as you have seen him
> *Being Transformed* into the heavens!'
> ¹²They turned to Jerusalem, back from the mountain
> That is called the Olive Mount,
> That is near Jerusalem, a Sabbath day's journey away.

The original Greek text of this account by the Evangelist Luke of what we usually call the Ascension of Christ, is pervaded by a flowing, compelling rhythm, as in one great and freely-drawn breath. We can feel how it appears to speak directly to us; how the speaker seems to be relating a direct experience, and that it is not merely a historical document.

The person by the name of Theophilus (friend of God), addressed in verse 1, is also the recipient of the first book of Luke, the Gospel. At the same time, the term 'friend of God' is so eloquent in its implied openness that everyone who encounters these words, may feel themselves addressed.

I would first like to draw attention to two of the italicised passages of the translation. In verse 3, we read that the Risen One appeared to the disciples during the forty days, and that in this period 'he spoke of "that" about the Kingdom of God'. In the Greek, this small τα *(ta)* 'that' is a neutral plural meaning 'all of that' or a 'plenitude'. This is clearly emphasised, but is ignored in most translations. The words of the Risen One are usually translated merely as speaking 'about the Kingdom of God' without referring to the mysterious 'that, all that', which is so pregnant with significance. Only a few English translations take account of this 'that' including the King James Bible where it is formulated as 'speaking of the things pertaining to the kingdom of God.'

Could it be that this small τα – 'all that' attempts to imply *all that* which is ineffable in this Kingdom? Is it comparable to the custom in Judaism of not speaking the name of God, since there is no name that is capable of bearing the depths and abundance of the being of God? Thus, the secret of the inner experience of the Kingdom of God may similarly be merely implied since there are no words that can encompass it.

Also, the word *exousia* in verse 7 is interesting for the translation if it is taken literally. For the most part, this passage is translated (correctly according to the dictionary) that God alone has the 'power' or 'authority' *(εξουσια, exousia)* to determine 'times and moments'. Man's will to knowledge is thereby repulsed and is subservient to the 'power', the omnipotence of God. Now *exousia* literally means: 'out of the essence, out of being'. In this the intrinsic tenor of the word *exousia*, Christ's answer to the disciples contains an allusion to the creative forming power of God.

An echo of the spirit of this word *exousia* is to be found in the descriptions of the heavenly hierarchy of the *Exousiai,* from the teachings of Dionysus the Areopagite in which they are creating, formative spirit powers.[1]

The free-flowing breathing rhythm of the text is made in the

Greek by the repeated use of the word 'and ... and', and above by the grammatical use of the participle form (see 'Grammar' in the Introduction). A translation into a modern European language cannot simply adopt the participle form without forcing the meaning. Therefore, in order to call attention to the living, constant movement of the breath, I have repeatedly emphasised such participle forms by using italics.

These manifold disparate forms of the participle express something like a process – something developing, something becoming that leads to openness; it is in movement, and invites us into this movement.

It appears to me that especially this Ascension text contains such a remarkable accord of form and content.

It is this open and *moved* quality, revealed in the abundant use of the participle form, which is commensurate to its content. It concerns the *movement of Christ* from the earth into the clouds (verse 9), and that the disciples – and with them the readers and hearers of the gospel – participate in this movement.

We are of course accustomed to speak of the *Ascension* of Christ, but the Greek text states something quite different and enlightening. The movement of Christ into the dimension of the heavens is literally described as 'to change, walk, wander, go', but not as ascension. This lends the entire event a very different character. 'To change' implies a wholly distinctive activity from an ascension.

This going 'into the heavens' by the transforming Christ, is directly experienced by the disciples in a sphere and consciousness outside time and space. It is deepened within them by the word of the angels. These divine messengers – as described in the previous chapter – do not promise a Parousia as a return of Christ in some distant time, but express how human beings will see Christ: wandering, metamorphosing, and thereby connecting earth and the heavens together 'in the same way' (verse 11) as the apostles had just witnessed.

After receiving the grace of this spiritual vision from the elevated position of the mountain (verse 12), as the text is at pains to point out, the people return to their everyday world, to working together, and to prayer 'in one mind' (Acts 1:14).

Thus, through the words of the angels, we discover in this text a similar story to that of the two disciples going to Emmaus, namely an indication of the Parousia as the presence of Christ and his gesture of accompanying.

Perhaps, to do justice to the nature of the event as interpreted here, we should speak of a 'heaven-wandering', rather than an ascension, with all its implications of escalation and soaring away. In the Creed of The Christian Community, we hear of the 'Lord of the heavenly forces on earth', which intimates this union *now* of the heavens and the earth.

To recognise and experience Christ in this way requires that the eye of the soul is opened. This comes through spiritual striving and ultimately through grace.

People will have to exchange the spirit of mere thinking
for the spirit of direct vision, of direct compassion and
shared experience of the Christ who is spiritually alive and
walks at the side of all human souls.[2]

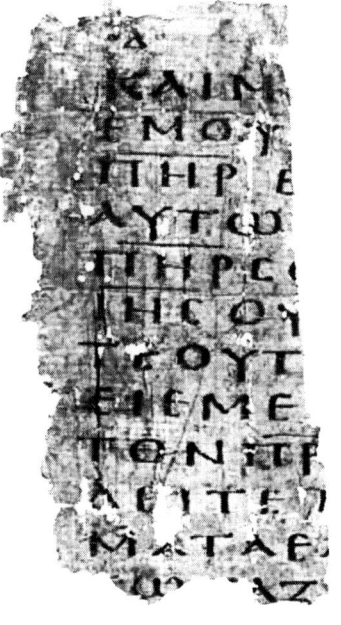

Καὶ ἐν τῷ συμπληροῦσθαι τὴν ἡμέραν τῆς Πεντεκοστῆς
ἦσαν πάντες ὁμοθυμαδὸν ἐπὶ τὸ αὐτό·
²καὶ ἐγένετο ἄφνω ἐκ τοῦ οὐρανοῦ ἦχος
ὥσπερ φερομένης πνοῆς βιαίας
καὶ ἐπλήρωσεν ὅλον τὸν οἶκον οὗ ἦσαν καθήμενοι,
³καὶ ὤφθησαν αὐτοῖς
διαμεριζόμεναι γλῶσσαι ὡσεὶ πυρός,
καὶ ἐκάθισεν ἐφ᾽ ἕνα ἕκαστον αὐτῶν,
⁴καὶ ἐπλήσθεσαν πάντες Πνεύματος Ἁγίου,
καὶ ἤρξαντο λαλεῖν ἑτέραις γλώσσαις
καθὼς τὸ Πνεῦμα ἐδίδου ἀποφθέγγεσθαι αὐτοῖς.
⁵Ἦσαν δὲ εἰς Ἱερουσαλὴμ κατοικοῦντες Ἰουδαῖοι,
ἄνδρες εὐλαβεῖς ἀπὸ παντὸς ἔθνους τῶν ὑπὸ τὸν
    οὐρανόν.

Whitsun

Tongues, divided, as of fire

The Whitsun event and the feminine Holy Spirit
(Acts 2:1–12)

In his *Italian Journey* Goethe describes how he experienced a Whitsun festival of different languages in Rome. One after the other thirty young people read the scriptures in their mother tongue – in Turkish, Persian, Arabic, Ethiopian, Syrian, etc. 'The Greek, however,' wrote Goethe, 'sounded like a star in the night.'

If we further explore the meaning of words and the grammatical forms of the original Greek in the Whitsun story, then new dimensions of its import may be revealed.

> And in the *becoming fulfilled* of the days of the *fifty*
> They were all *unanimous* in their *self*.
> ²And it happened suddenly, an *echo* resounded out of the heavens
> Like a mighty *spirit* rushing in
> And filled the entire house, where they sat in anticipation.
> ³And it was perceived by them
> *Tongues, divided, as of fire*
> And they settled on each one of them.
> ⁴And they were all filled with the *Holy Spirit*,
> And began to speak in *other tongues*
> As the spirit gave them to *raise* their voice.
> ⁵Now there lived in Jerusalem Jews,
> Devoted men from all nations under heaven

⁶γενομένης δὲ τῆς φωνῆς ταύτης
συνῆλθεν τὸ πλῆθος καὶ συνεχύθη,
ὅτι ἤκουον εἷς ἕκαστος τῇ ἰδίᾳ διαλέκτῳ λαλούντων
   αὐτῶν·
⁷ἐξίσταντο δὲ καὶ ἐθαύμαζον
λέγοντες·
Οὐχ ἰδοὺ
πάντες οὗτοί εἰσιν οἱ λαλοῦντες Γαλιλαῖοι;
⁸καὶ πῶς ἡμεῖς ἀκούομεν ἕκαστος τῇ ἰδίᾳ διαλέκτῳ ἡμῶν
ἐν ᾗ ἐγεννήθημεν;
⁹Πάρθοι καὶ Μῆδοι καὶ Ἐλαμῖται,
καὶ οἱ κατοικοῦντες τὴν Μεσοποταμίαν, Ἰουδαίαν
τε καὶ Καππαδοκίαν, Πόντον καὶ τὴν Ἀσίαν,
¹⁰Φρυγίαν τε καὶ Παμφυλίαν, Αἴγυπτον
καὶ τὰ μέρη τῆς Λιβύης τῆς κατὰ Κυρήνην,
καὶ οἱ ἐπιδημοῦντες Ῥωμαῖοι,
¹¹Ἰουδαῖοί τε καὶ προσήλυτοι, Κρῆτες καὶ Ἄραβες,
ἀκούομεν λαλούντων αὐτῶν
ταῖς ἡμετέραις γλώσσαις τὰ μεγαλεῖα τοῦ Θεοῦ;
¹²ἐξίσταντο δὲ πάντες καὶ διηποροῦντο,
ἄλλος πρὸς ἄλλον λέγοντες·
Τί θέλει τοῦτο εἶναι;

⁶As this voice happened,
The crowd came together and became confused
As each one of them heard them speak in his own tongue.
⁷They were beside themselves and full of astonishment
And cried:
'No, see,
Are not all these who speak here Galileans?
⁸And how is it that we each hear our own language
Into which we have been born?
⁹Parthians and Medes and Elamites
And inhabitants of Mesopotamia, Judea,
And also Cappadocia, Pontus and Asia,
¹⁰Phrygia and Pamphylia, people from Egypt,
Libya and Cyrene,
Romans who have settled here,
¹¹Jews and proselytes, Cretans and Arabians –
We hear them in our language
Speaking of the great deeds of God.'
¹²All were beside themselves, they were at a loss
And they said to one another,
'What will become of this?'

Let us follow the trail of a few words that are italicised.

The text begins with a grammatical form, which expresses boundlessness: the 'becoming fulfilled' συμπληρουσθαι *(symplērousthai)* is a nominalised infinitive in the passive. An infinitive is, as its name 'in-finis' suggests, a form without end, without bounds. It is good to stumble a little over this eloquent grammatical verb form, without attempting to immediately correct it with a more aesthetically pleasing phrasing, such as 'Since the day of Pentecost had come ...' For through this grammatical form of the nominalised infinitive ('becoming fulfilled') from the very beginning the story has a boundlessness, opening up a space through which the reader can enter.

The number in verse 1, *fifty*, – the meaning of Pentecost – contains something hidden. There was a long-established Jewish festival, Shavuot, long before the Christian Whitsun which was celebrated fifty days, or seven weeks after the Jewish Passover. This was a harvest festival, in which bread from the newly harvested crops was eaten. Since in Hebrew the signs for the letters are at the same time signs for numbers, we find that fifty is represented by the letter *nun,* which means *fish*. The number fifty and the letter *nun* were always heard, felt and understood as a single whole. There is also another aspect to the fish hidden in the number fifty. Jehoshua (Joshua) who, after Moses' death, led the people of Israel into the promised land, is called in the Old Testament 'son of Nun', son of the Fish. Jehoshua is in fact the Hebrew form of the name Jesus. Both Jehoshuas, Joshua and Jesus Christ, lead man into a promised land. And the fish was used as a symbol for Christ in the early days of Christianity.

Also the word 'unanimous' *(ὁμοθυμαδον, homothumadon)* in verse 1, is particularly expressive. From the many textual variants I have chosen 'unanimous' for this translation. Precisely the same word is used just a few verses before to characterise the people gathered together after the Ascension, when they 'were in *unanimous* worship'. Those named include the disciples, the women, the brothers of Jesus, and expressly named, his mother, Mary (Acts 1:14). This use of *ὁμοθυμαδον (homothumadon),* implies that the people were all there in 'common thymos'. *Thymos* was experienced by the Greek as a special sphere, as the centre of a person, the physical-psychological sphere of thinking, feeling and will. At the same time with this form the unanimous being-together, the common longing in worship, the text emphasises the individuality of each one: 'in their self', *ἐπι το αὐτο (epi to auto)*. The expression can be understood in two ways: as an allusion to the place of their gathering (probably the same location as the Last Supper), 'in their own (place)'; and it can connote an inner place, in the sense of being 'by oneself' or 'coming to oneself'.

The word 'echo' *ἠχος (ēchos,* verse 2), which has been directly integrated into many European languages, refers to a decisive moment in the Whitsun story. Could it be that not so much a 'rushing' is meant – as 'echo' has usually been translated, and which has taken a firm hold of the collective imagination – but rather an *echo* resounding out of the heavens? Is it not more of an overwhelming sounding, a powerful resonance, an *acknowledgment* to the people gathered in unanimous worship?

The formulation in verse 3, 'tongues, divided, as from fire' – διαμεριζόμεναι γλῶσσαι ὡσεὶ πυρὸς *(diamerizomenai glōssai hōsei pyros)* – completes the picture. The primal universal fire of the spirit becomes visible in *single* flames above each individual person. This spirit primal fire, experienced in the unanimity of this special community, unfolds in each individual a new comprehension and capacity to speak. This event is characterised in verse 4 with the words 'in other tongues ... to raise their voice' λαλεῖν ἑτέραις γλώσσαις *(lalein heterais glōssais)*, to speak and understand in the speech of others. There unfolded a new form of speaking, directly out of the received Spirit.

Furthermore, the way that the Holy Spirit appears in the Pentecostal story is also remarkable. In verse 2 it appears with the words 'mighty spirit' πνοῆς βιαίας *(pnoēs biaias)*. Astonishingly, it is not called τὸ πνεῦμα *(to pneuma),* the otherwise common neutral form, which envelops the wide significance of 'spirit, breath, wind, air' and which appears in this form in the New Testament approximately 340 times. Rather we read here of a *feminine* form that occurs just twice in the New Testament and which also means 'spirit, breath, wind, and air': ἡ πνοη *(hē pnoē)*.[1] The question naturally arises whether the original Greek text, in using this conspicuous form at this point, is trying to draw attention to a feminine Holy Spirit.

Although unquestionably, the neutral form for the Spirit is the more common (see also verse 4), there is nonetheless a feminine form in Greek, and when it is used, we can be sure that there is a good reason for it. But what reason exactly?

The Old Testament speaks self-evidently about this divine feminine aspect. In many texts, the feminine appears as complementary to the masculine principle. Both work together as a

²²יְהוָה קָנָנִי רֵאשִׁית דַּרְכּוֹ
קֶדֶם מִפְעָלָיו מֵאָז:
²³מֵעוֹלָם נִסַּכְתִּי
מֵרֹאשׁ מִקַּדְמֵי־אָרֶץ:
²⁴בְּאֵין־תְּהֹמוֹת חוֹלָלְתִּי
בְּאֵין מַעְיָנוֹת נִכְבַּדֵּי־מָיִם
²⁵בְּטֶרֶם הָרִים הָטְבָּעוּ לִפְנֵי גְבָעוֹת
חוֹלָלְתִּי:
²⁶עַד־לֹא עָשָׂה אֶרֶץ וְחוּצוֹת
וְרֹאשׁ עָפְרוֹת תֵּבֵל:
²⁷בַּהֲכִינוֹ שָׁמַיִם שָׁם אָנִי
בְּחוּקוֹ חוּג עַל־פְּנֵי תְהוֹם:
²⁸בְּאַמְּצוֹ שְׁחָקִים מִמָּעַל
בַּעֲזוֹז עִינוֹת תְּהוֹם:
²⁹בְּשׂוּמוֹ לַיָּם חֻקּוֹ
וּמַיִם לֹא יַעַבְרוּ־פִיו
בְּחוּקוֹ מוֹסְדֵי אָרֶץ:
³⁰וָאֶהְיֶה אֶצְלוֹ אָמוֹן
וָאֶהְיֶה שַׁעֲשֻׁעִים יוֹם יוֹם מְשַׂחֶקֶת לְפָנָיו בְּכָל־עֵת:
³¹מְשַׂחֶקֶת בְּתֵבֵל אַרְצוֹ
וְשַׁעֲשֻׁעַי אֶת־בְּנֵי אָדָם:

creative spirit of God. For this reason, we can discard any superficial interpretations of the male/female aspects.

Already in Genesis, there is an expression for the world-creating spirit of God, רוּחַ אֱלֹהִים *(ruach Elohim)*, which in Hebrew is a feminine word. In this context, in the wisdom literature of the Old Testament, a feminine aspect of the divine is named, *Chokhma*.[2] She is the living, creating active wisdom. In Greek, she is called *Sophia*. There is a multitude of passages which concern this creative aspect of the Chokhma/Sophia/wisdom, although she comprises many other qualities as well.[3]

The Chokhma/Sophia/wisdom is the divine immanence and accomplice to the creation of worlds since the very beginning. In the Book of Proverbs (8:22–31) she says of herself:

> [22]I was with Yahweh at the beginnings of his paths
> Before his works, always
> [23]From eternities I have come
> From the beginning, before the earth,
> [24]Before the flood I was born
> When there were no springs abounding with water
> [25]Before the mountains were set, before the hills –
> I was born
> [26]Then, he had not yet made land and field
> Nor yet the first dust of the earth
> [27]As he created the heavens, I was there,
> When he measured a circle over the face of the deep,
> [28]As he made firm the clouds above
> As he made strong the springs of the deep,
> [29]As he set his limit to the sea
> So that the waters might not transgress his bounds
> As he laid the foundations of the earth,
> [30]*There I was, beside him, his master-builder*[4]
> I was from day to day his delight, dancing before him always
> [31]Played on his earth
> And my joy was with the sons of man.

In this great and image-rich hymnal text, the Chokhma/Sophia/wisdom reveals herself as deeply affiliated to the divine world-creation. Her self-description as master builder characterises her clearly as an active participant of this creating. Her dancing, playing levity and joy pervades every single step of the creation in Genesis. She reflects also the enthusiasm which is to be found in all genuine creative processes.

The creative feminine aspect of the Spirit deepens again into the Christian figure of Mary. From the very beginnings of Christianity, she was perceived as the embodiment of Sophia. She is often represented as sitting on the 'throne of Wisdom'. In many paintings of the Pentecostal event, she is given special prominence. Thus Mary is the inner centre of the company of the disciples. In her radiant majesty, Chokhma/Sophia has become human.

Thus in the account of Whitsun we have the most comprehensive revelation of the Holy Spirit which includes the feminine aspect of the creative divinity.

As a result of my intensive musings on the text of Whitsun, I wrote a poem.

Whitsun

Fulfilled are the days of the waiting,
Fulfilled the fifty,
To break the bread of the new harvest
We wait.

Son of Nun
Jehoshua,
Led into the land,
The promised,

And then the OTHER,
Walking further
Until the end of times.

Suddenly,
There!
Piercing through time
Out of heaven-dew
Space creating,
Opening,
In the storm wind's
Transforming.

And wind-fire-forces
Like flame-lights
On every single
Head.

Tentative voices
Speak,
Language
Born
To understand anew.

St John's Tide

He must increase, I must decrease

John the Baptist (Mark 1:1–12)

Ἐκεῖνον δεῖ αὐξάνειν, ἐμὲ δὲ ἐλαττοῦσθαι.
He must increase, but I must decrease (John 3:30).

Also during the period of St John's Tide, the living presence of the Old Testament in the New Testament can be clearly felt. Its diverse messages reaching out over the millennia end with the words of the prophet Malachi which resonate like a direct bridge to the New Testament.

הִנְנִי שֹׁלֵחַ מַלְאָכִי וּפִנָּה־דֶרֶךְ לְפָנָי
Behold, I send my angel, and he will prepare the path before my countenance (Mal.3:1).

הִנֵּה אָנֹכִי שֹׁלֵחַ לָכֶם אֵת אֵלִיָּה הַנָּבִיא לִפְנֵי בּוֹא יוֹם יְהוָה הַגָּדוֹל וְהַנּוֹרָא
Behold, I send you Elijah, the prophet, before the day of the I AM, the great and radiant, fear-inspiring day[1] (Mal.4:5).

Mark begins his gospel with the appearance of John. His role as preparer of the path of the Messiah had been announced by the Jewish prophets. Already in the second sentence Mark quotes Malachi, then Isaiah (40:3), and then names the messenger, John the Baptist (Mark 1:4).

Ἀρχὴ τοῦ εὐαγγελίου Ἰησοῦ Χριστοῦ, Υἱοῦ Θεοῦ.
²Καθὼς γέγραπται ἐν τῷ Ἠσαΐᾳ τῷ προφήτῃ·
Ἰδοὺ
ἀποστέλλω τὸν ἄγγελόν μου πρὸ προσώπου σου,
ὃς κατασκευάσει τὴν ὁδόν σου·
³φωνὴ βοῶντος ἐν τῇ ἐρήμῳ·
Ἑτοιμάσατε
τὴν ὁδὸν Κυρίου,
εὐθείας ποιεῖτε τὰς τρίβους αὐτοῦ,
⁴ἐγένετο Ἰωάννης ὁ βαπτίζων ἐν τῇ ἐρήμῳ
κηρύσσων βάπτισμα μετανοίας
εἰς ἄφεσιν ἁμαρτιῶν·
⁵καὶ ἐξεπορεύετο πρὸς αὐτὸν πᾶσα ἡ Ἰουδαία χώρα
καὶ οἱ Ἱεροσολυμῖται πάντες,
καὶ ἐβαπτίζοντο ὑπ' αὐτοῦ ἐν τῷ Ἰορδάνῃ ποταμῷ
ἐξομολογούμενοι τὰς ἁμαρτίας αὐτῶν·
⁶καὶ ἦν ὁ Ἰωάννης ἐνδεδυμένος
τρίχας καμήλου
καὶ ζώνην δερματίνην περὶ τὴν ὀσφὺν αὐτοῦ,
καὶ ἐσθίων ἀκρίδας καὶ μέλι ἄγριον·
⁷καὶ ἐκήρυσσεν λέγων·

The name of John also directs us to a connection between the Old and New Testaments. In Hebrew, the name of God Yahweh is contained in John, so that John can be translated as 'the I-AM is grace'. The proclamation 'I AM THE I AM' was the name that the God Yahweh made himself known by, when at the burning bush Moses asked him for his name (Exod.3:13f). The extraordinary figure of John the Baptist appears in all four gospels, in the Koran and is mentioned by the historian Josephus.[2]

We shall follow the text from the beginning of Mark's Gospel.

Beginning of the gospel of Jesus Christ, the Son of God.
[2]As it is written by Isaiah the prophet:
'Behold,
I send my angel before your countenance,
Who will prepare for you a path.
[3]A voice of one calling in the desert:
Prepare, now
The way of the I AM
Make straight his paths.'
[4]John, the Baptising one, appeared into the desert
And he preached a baptism of changing heart and mind,
Which would free from sins.
[5]And there came out to him from the whole land of Judea,
And there came all of the people of Jerusalem
And were baptised by him in the Jordan river,
And they spoke out all of their separation.
[6]Dressed was John with a cloak
From the hair of camels
And he wore a belt, leather, around his waist
And he ate *locusts and the honey of wild bees.*
[7]He proclaimed and spoke:

Ἔρχεται
ὁ ἰσχυρότερός μου
ὀπίσω μου,
οὗ οὐκ εἰμὶ ἱκανὸς κύψας
λῦσαι τὸν ἱμάντα τῶν ὑποδημάτων αὐτοῦ·
⁸ἐγὼ
ἐβάπτισα ὑμᾶς ὕδατι,·
αὐτὸς δὲ
βαπτίσει ὑμᾶς ἐν Πνεύματι Ἁγίῳ.
⁹Καὶ ἐγένετο ἐν ἐκείναις ταῖς ἡμέραις
ἦλθεν Ἰησοῦς ἀπὸ Ναζαρὲθ τῆς Γαλιλαίας
καὶ ἐβαπτίσθη εἰς τὸν Ἰορδάνην ὑπὸ Ἰωάννου·
¹⁰καὶ εὐθὺς ἀναβαίνων ἐκ τοῦ ὕδατος
εἶδεν σχιζομένους τοὺς οὐρανοὺς
καὶ τὸ Πνεῦμα ὡς περιστερὰν
καταβαῖνον εἰς αὐτόν·
¹¹καὶ φωνὴ ἐγένετο ἐκ τῶν οὐρανῶν·
Σὺ
εἶ ὁ Υἱός μου ὁ ἀγαπητός,
ἐν σοὶ εὐδόκησα.

> 'He is coming,
> He, the one who is stronger than I
> After me,
> To whom I am not worthy to bend down
> To untie the thong of his sandals.
> ⁸I,
> I baptise you with water
> But he,
> He will baptise you with the Holy Spirit.'
> ⁹And it happened in those days:
> Jesus came from Nazareth in Galilee
> And he was baptised by John in the Jordan river.
> ¹⁰And immediately, as he came up out of the water
> John saw the heavens opening
> And the Spirit like a dove
> Descend in him,
> ¹¹And a voice rang out of the heavens:
> 'You,
> You are my son, my beloved,
> In you I reveal myself.'

This beginning of the Gospel of Mark reads like a great hymn, rejoicing in the proclamation. Familiar words and images from Old Testament prophets are woven into a new announcement. The repetitious style of the original Greek text (which for us may appear to be superfluous), such as 'he, he' (verses 7, 8), 'I, I' (verse 8) and 'you, you' (verse 11), as well as the frequent use of 'and' belong to the style of the text and emphasise the urgency of the message.

The pithy description gives an unforgettable image of this outstanding prophet, John the Baptist. Even the description of his clothing and food, otherwise a neglected detail in the gospels, is expressly mentioned.

Locusts and the honey of wild bees (verse 6): To this day, commentators are divided on the meaning of the highly peculiar fare of locusts that the Baptist apparently indulged in. Suggested text changes instead of ἀκρίδες *(akrides,* locusts) are ἀχαρίδες, καρίδες *(acharides, karides,* the tips of herbs) or ἀχράδες *(achrades,* wild pears), or the more distant Hebrew חרוב *charub,* carob tree.[3] But all of these are merely speculation. Admittedly, one would have to change every occurrence of the well-verified word ἀκρίς *(akris)* meaning 'locust' in the most important extant scrolls.[4] But since according to the strict Jewish dietary laws the locust was pure (Lev.11:22), we may perhaps safely put the 'locust problem' to one side.

In the description of the John's apparel (verse 6), there is an obvious (for Mark's contemporaries) allusion to the prophet Elijah whose return before the advent of the Messiah had been foretold. The dress of John and Elijah are in fact described with the same words:

'A man with a cloak made from camel-hair and a belt of leather around the waist' (2Kings 1:8). In a time and world in which agnosticism was unknown, and when the Holy Scriptures pervaded all aspects of daily life, such words found immediate resonance amongst their hearers. The imminent arrival of the Messiah, which had been prophesied through the centuries, was expected with immense longing. The return of Elijah was the requisite condition for this. So it is understandable that the priests and Levites ask John whether he was Elijah (John 1:21).

The deep connection between the individuality of John the Baptist with the prophet Elijah is demonstrated by the words of Christ in a discussion with the disciples which occurs after the events of the Transfiguration on Mount Tabor:

And the disciples asked him, 'Why do the scribes say that first Elijah must come?' He replied and spoke, 'Yes Elijah does come and will restore all. But I say to you, *Elijah has come,* but they have not recognised him, but have done to him what they wanted. So also the Son of Man will suffer through them.' *And they understood that he spoke of John the Baptist* to them (Matt.17:10–13).

And in another passage it says: 'And if you can accept it, he *is Elijah, who will come*. He who has ears to hear, let him hear.' (Matt.11:14f and similarly Mark 9:11–13).

The intensity with which John-Elijah assumes his task as the forerunner and preparer of the path of Christ, is revealed in how he is the only one who recognises Jesus of Nazareth as the long-anticipated Messiah, the Christ, and his universal task (verses 7 and 8). John also lives in the sphere of inspiration and can hear the divine voice that resounds through the opening heavens (verse 11).

Mark's very first sentence, 'Beginning of the gospel of Jesus Christ, the Son of God' imparts some of the urgency, typical of the character of his text. Reading him aloud, his voice sounds like a far-resounding fanfare, creating with rhythm and power a bridge from the prophetic voices of Malachi and Isaiah.

We can ask ourselves what it was like at the time of Mark, when an old text, so familiar from being read and heard in the synagogues for centuries, appeared in something new. The modern term for this is quoting. But for those hearing these words at the beginnings of Christianity, the experience was far deeper, perhaps something like a re-encounter with familiar prophetic words which now found their place in their own time and began to take on a new life. Mark quotes the words of Isaiah, who had given King Hezekiah the prophetic good tidings of the return of the people of Israel from the Babylonian exile. And this now sounds together with the *new* good tidings of Jesus Christ and his forerunner John.

Every pious Jew at the time of Christ knew the following text from Isaiah (40:1–5) by heart, whose words from verse 3 are woven into Mark's text:

נַחֲמוּ נַחֲמוּ עַמִּי
יֹאמַר אֱלֹהֵיכֶם:
²דַּבְּרוּ עַל־לֵב יְרוּשָׁלַם וְקִרְאוּ אֵלֶיהָ
כִּי מָלְאָה צְבָאָהּ
כִּי נִרְצָה עֲוֺנָהּ
כִּי לָקְחָה מִיַּד יְהוָה
כִּפְלַיִם בְּכָל־חַטֹּאתֶיהָ:
³קוֹל קוֹרֵא
בַּמִּדְבָּר פַּנּוּ דֶּרֶךְ יְהוָה
יַשְּׁרוּ בָּעֲרָבָה מְסִלָּה לֵאלֹהֵינוּ:
⁴כָּל־גֶּיא יִנָּשֵׂא
וְכָל־הַר וְגִבְעָה יִשְׁפָּלוּ
וְהָיָה הֶעָקֹב לְמִישׁוֹר
וְהָרְכָסִים לְבִקְעָה
⁵וְנִגְלָה כְּבוֹד יְהוָה
וְרָאוּ כָל־בָּשָׂר יַחְדָּו
כִּי פִּי יְהוָה
דִּבֵּר:

> Console, console my people
> Speaks your God-Elohim
> ²Speaks to the hearts of Jerusalem and calls her
> That her desolation is complete,
> Her guilt atoned,
> That she has received from the hand of the I-AM
> Double in all her separation.
> ³*A voice calls:*
> *In the desert prepare a way for the I-AM*
> *Level in the wilderness a road for our God-Elohim!*
> ⁴Every valley will raise itself,
> Mountain and hill will sink low
> And the crooked will become straight
> And the rugged become wide plains
> ⁵The revelation of the I-AM will be unveiled
> And all things living will perceive HIM
> For the mouth of the I-AM
> Has spoken.

Even today the dual nature of this text can sound for us in a way that goes beyond a mere ascertainment that we are hearing a 'quotation' from the Old Testament in the New. The words of comfort spoken 2500 years ago by Isaiah in a historical situation, and the appeal by John to prepare a way in the desert of the soul reverberate together in two autonomous voices.

In this weaving together of gospel and the Isaiah text, something new, something beyond time, begins to evolve which is current and can be grasped in the moment that it is heard or read. This corresponds to what Origen termed the 'moral sense'. This is the sense which stands above the important historical level of understanding the text, and concerns itself more with the existential question, what does this mean to me?

The spiritual or rising sense goes even further than this, attempting to place the text into its great spiritual context. And we find that in this question of the I AM a far more profound connection exists between the two parts of the Bible. Christ

אֶהְיֶה אֲשֶׁר אֶהְיֶה

Ὁ Πατήρ μου, ἕως ἄρτι ἐργάζεται, κἀγὼ ἐργάζομαι

Ἐγὼ καὶ ὁ Πατὴρ ἕν ἐσμεν.

Καθὼς σύ, Πατήρ, ἐν ἐμοὶ κἀγὼ ἐν σοί, ἵνα καὶ αὐτοὶ ἐν ἡμῖν ὦσιν, ἵνα ὁ κόσμος πιστεύῃ ὅτι σύ με ἀπέστειλας· κἀγὼ τὴν δόξαν ἥν δέδωκάς μοι δέωκα αὐτοῖς, ἵνα ὦσιν ἕν καθὸς ἡμεῖς ἕν.

[Χριστός] ἐστιν εἰκὼν τοῦ Θεοῦ τοῦ ἀοράτου, πρωτότοκος πάσης κτίσεως.

describes himself twelve times in the Gospel of John as the I AM, directly recalling the words of Yahweh in the burning bush:[5]

> I AM THE I AM (Exod.3:14).

Further self-characterisations by The Christ assume the same direction:

> My father is working until now, I myself am now working (John 5:17).

> I and the Father are one (John 10:30).

> As you, Father, are in me, and I am in you, they also should be in us, so that the world knows, that you have sent me. And I have given them the revelation-glory, that you gave me: for they should be one, as we are one. (John 17:21f).

And Paul spoke in this manner to the Colossians:

> [Christ], the image of the invisible god, the first born of the entire creation (Col.1:15).

Rudolf Steiner's elucidation has shone a unique light on this connection, which brings us to fundamental questions on the nature of world evolution and the Trinity. Its significance, however, will provoke further questions which must ripen over a lifetime.

> And you can understand the Old or the New Testament only if you know that the God proclaimed by Moses is the Christ who was ... to walk among people ... The members of the Hebrew mystery centres knew it; they worshipped the Christ and recognized him as the speaker of the words, 'Tell my people: *I am the I am.*'[6]

Michaelmas

The armour of God

Paul's Letter to the Ephesians (Ephesians 6:10–18)

Who was Paul?

'One of the people of Israel, from the tribe of Benjamin, a Hebrew amongst Hebrews, according to the Law, a Pharisee.' In this fashion, Paul writes about himself in the Letter to the Philippians (3:5). A proud acknowledgment of his Hebrew identity – but he writes this declaration in the Greek language. As a Jew of the Diaspora, Paul was a citizen of three worlds: the Jewish, the Greek-Hellenistic, and the Roman. He was born far from Jerusalem, in Tarsus, now in Turkey. Paul had the Hebrew name of the first Israelite king שאול, Shaul, 'the one who is asked' (Saulus in Latin). He was educated in Greek and imbued the Hellenic culture of his time. As was the custom amongst educated Jews at the time, he also learnt a trade. His craft was tent-making (Acts 18:3). Since birth and circumcision, Paul was also known by his Greek name, *Παυλος (Paulos,* the small one). An additional name was common practice amongst Jews in the Roman Empire. In the Acts of the Apostles, which is the main source of our knowledge of the life and work of Paul, both names are referred to, 'Saul [Shaul], who is also called Paul' (Acts 13:9).

Koine Greek, the language of his time and world, was his mother tongue.[1] He would have been familiar with Latin as a citizen of a Roman province, even if merely in legal contexts. Hebrew and the Hebrew dialect of Aramaic were the languages which he spoke in the synagogue, and in his daily prayers. By virtue of his different languages, he is capable of penetrating the different mentalities and outlooks of the many other peoples of the Roman Empire (called Gentiles in the New Testament). Thus Paul is predestined to preach the gospel of Jesus Christ to his own people, the Jews, and to the Gentiles. He himself said of this: to the Jew, a Jew, to the Greeks, a Greek, to be all things to all men (1Cor.9:19f). One need only call to mind how he addressed the Athenians in public on the Areopagus with the idea of the 'unknown God' and the resurrection. Moving freely in their language and culture, he quoted Greek poets (Acts 17:28).

The Jews of Tarsus were purposely settled there under Antiochus IV Epiphanes (215–164 BC), and enjoyed a privileged status being granted the valuable legal status of a Roman citizenship, which gave them the legal right to a trial and protection of their life. Paul, as reported in Acts, was born a Roman citizen (Acts 21:39, 22:25–29). This several times saved his life on his extensive journeys to disseminate his message of the Resurrection of Jesus Christ.

Paul went to Jerusalem as a young man for a strict religious education and schooling. He became a pupil of the famous Rabbi Gamaliel the Elder (died AD 50).[2] Here he became a scholar and a Pharisee who lived in accord with the strict laws of the 613 mitzvot (the commandments of the Torah), of which the Ten Commandments are only part. It was thus a man highly schooled in religion and culture who encountered the Risen Christ in the event before Damascus. It became a deeply transforming experience that shook Paul to the very core of his being.

The initiation experience of Damascus

Paul was a man full of the fire of spirit. Unlike reading the gospels, when we read Paul's epistles we can immediately discern a human personality behind the writing. His was a personality which was human in its variety, incongruities, struggles, cares, doubts, anger, empathy, and in his love. In his manner of speech and thought, we find an original and wilful character.

Through Paul's widely promulgating the message of the Risen Christ, Christianity no longer remained a matter among a small circle of disciples in Jerusalem, but became a world affair. The origin of this impulse which continues to this day is to be found in the experience of Damascus.[3] This turned Paul from being a cruel and fanatical opponent of the first Christians – who in his eyes were nothing more than apostate Jews deserving the penalty of death – into an ardent evangelist of the Resurrected Christ.

In his letters, Paul always speaks directly out of the centre of his being into the depths of the experience of the Christ transformation. Just how central this Damascus experience was for him may be ascertained by the fact that it is mentioned no less than seven times in his letters and the Acts.[4]

In all cultures of the ancient world we find the mysteries with their fabled initiations. These were directed by masters (hierophants) whose teaching methods included strict exercises of the body and of the spirit. In this way the hierophants led the neophytes to an experience of the divine, and thus to a new consciousness beyond the everyday. Since the discovery of the Qumran and the Nag Hamadi scrolls in 1947 and 1949, there has been a general consensus in theological circles that there must also have been a Jewish mystery centre with a corresponding esoteric teaching and schooling.[5] What is exceptional about Paul's initiation experience is that he reports it taking place without a human master directing it.

Rudolf Steiner referred to this and emphasised that Paul was the first example of an initiation without the working of a hierophant.[6] This could indicate that what Paul experienced was the beginning of a change in the mysteries of the ancient world. A candidate would no longer have to be helped by a hierophant or initiate to follow the path to knowledge of higher worlds, but now Christ revealed himself as God descending to earth, appearing directly to the individual. Paul put this experience into words: 'If anyone is in Christ, then he is a new creation. The old has passed away, behold, the new has become.' (2Cor.5:17).

After his Damascus experience, the three days being blind and his baptism by Ananias in Damascus, Paul does not as a new convert immediately go to Jerusalem to the other apostles and eye-witnesses of the life of Christ. Rather, he withdraws for three years into 'Arabia' (Gal.1:17f).[7] With this somewhat imprecise location of Arabia, and the allusion to three years, may be a veiled reference to a time of complete transformation following the experience on the way to Damascus.

In this time Paul neither preached nor founded communities, and in contrast to his usually expansive reports on his travels, he remains silent about this time in Arabia. The basic meaning of the word 'Arabia' in Greek *(Ἀραβια, Arabia)* – as it is in Hebrew (ערבה, *'arabah)* is 'desert'. So the location that Paul refers to could be the desert, a place of absolute inward and external testing, a place of consciously chosen solitude and immense spiritual metamorphosis. Since Moses and the days of Elijah right up until Jesus Christ, the desert has always played such a crucial part. Paul's faith and outlook was founded on the initiation experience of the Risen Christ at Damascus and matured during the subsequent three years in 'Arabia'. This formed the basis for his three great missionary journeys. They led him over thousands of miles on foot and by ship, into many regions and cities of the Mediterranean stretching as far as the olive tree grows.

For Paul's Jewish audience in the synagogues which Paul first visited, his message was considered nothing less than scandalous. He indicated that the Christ who appeared to him was the crucified rabbi Jesus of Nazareth who rose from the dead, and who was the expected Messiah. To Jewish ears this was simply outrageous blasphemy. The reactions were corresponding: 'From the Jews five times I have received forty lashes less one; I was beaten with sticks three times, and once stoned' (2Cor.11:24f).

Paul's words make clear to us just how much indefatigable endurance and personal sacrifice was necessary on his part in order to spread his message. The experience at Damascus, as well as the later one in Jerusalem at the Temple when he saw the Risen One and was given the task to preach the gospel to the Gentiles (Acts 22), were the foundations upon which this enormous achievement was made possible.

His well-known and oft-quoted phrase, 'I live, no longer I, but rather in me lives Christ' (Gal.2:20), which he repeated in many variations refers clearly to this 'being in Christ' as the source of his life and of all of his work.[8] Paul speaks and preaches purely out of this revelation.

Although he was a contemporary of Jesus, Paul never saw him during his life. At the time of his activity, there were no written gospels. The disciples also found it extremely difficult to accept this stubborn and erstwhile opponent. He was accused of preaching a different gospel (Gal.1:6–10); and that his gospel caused obfuscation; and of twisting the word of God (2Cor.4:2f); and of having a different spirit (2Cor.11:4). Paul answered these accusations in the Letter to the Galatians, amongst others: 'For I have neither received it [the gospel] nor been taught it from any person, but through the revelation of Jesus Christ' (Gal.1:12).

The Letter to the Ephesians

It is claimed in the Letter to the Ephesians, that while imprisoned in Rome, Paul wrote it for the Christian communities founded by him in Ephesus (1:1; 3:1 & 6:20). However, in recent research on Paul, differences are seen in the letters believed to be written by Paul and those believed to originate from his closest followers, called the school of Paul. Romans, Galatians, Philippians and Philemon as well as the two Corinthian letters are seen as Paul's work, whereas the letter to the Ephesians is seen as the product of this school.[9]

In tackling the linguistic challenges of such a text as the Letter to the Ephesians, the question of whether it was written directly by Paul becomes somewhat academic. The language, style, content and process of thought of the Christian message have the mark of Paul. Thus the theologian Eugen Biser has concluded that the school of Paul 'continues the intuitions and thoughts of the apostle'.[10]

The impartial reader, however, comparing the different letters will be struck by a manifest continuity: like a musical keynote, Paul's experience of 'being in Christ' pervades the entire text.

Our passage concerns the 'armour of God'. It takes on a new character if the Letter to the Ephesians is seen as a *speech* directed at those *initiated* through the Christian Baptism.[11] Moreover it contains various known phrases from the mysteries: for instance with the idea of sealing: 'to be sealed with the Holy Spirit, which is promised' (1:13), or when the 'enlightened eyes of the heart' (1:18), the basis of the newly awakening form of cognition is spoken of. Or there is the description of how the dual human nature, previously separated from the divine can be united with Christ in the initiation of the Baptism: 'to create a new man out of the duality in himself' (2:15).

¹⁰Τοῦ λοιποῦ,
ἐνδυναμοῦσθε ἐν Κυρίῳ
καὶ ἐν τῷ κράτει τῆς ἰσχύος αὐτοῦ·
¹¹ἐνδύσασθε τὴν πανοπλίαν τοῦ θεοῦ
πρὸς τὸ δύνασθαι ὑμᾶς στῆναι
πρὸς τὰς μεθοδείας τοῦ διαβόλου·
¹²ὅτι οὐκ ἔστιν ἡμῖν
ἡ πάλη πρὸς αἷμα καὶ σάρκα,
ἀλλὰ πρὸς τὰς ἀρχάς,
πρὸς τὰς ἐξουσίας,
πρὸς τοὺς κοσμοκράτορας τοῦ σκότους τούτου,
πρὸς τὰ πνευματικὰ τῆς πονηρίας ἐν τοῖς ἐπουρανίοις·
¹³διὰ τοῦτο ἀναλάβετε τὴν πανοπλίαν τοῦ θεοῦ,
ἵνα δυνηθῆτε ἀντιστῆναι ἐν τῇ ἡμέρᾳ τῇ πονηρᾷ
καὶ ἅπαντα κατεργασάμενοι
στῆναι·
¹⁴στῆτε οὖν
περιζωσάμενοι τὴν ὀσφὺν ὑμῶν ἐν ἀληθείᾳ,
καὶ ἐνδυσάμενοι τὸν θώρακα τῆς δικαιοσύνης,
¹⁵καὶ ὑποδησάμενοι τοὺς πόδας ἐν ἑτοιμασίᾳ
τοῦ εὐαγγελίου τῆς εἰρήνης,
¹⁶ἐν πᾶσιν ἀναλαβόντες τὸν θυρεὸν τῆς πίστεως,
ἐν ᾧ δυνήσεσθε πάντα τὰ βέλη τοῦ πονηροῦ
τὰ πεπυρωμένα σβέσαι·
¹⁷καὶ τὴν περικεφαλαίαν τοῦ σωτηρίου δέξασθε,
καὶ τὴν μάχαιραν τοῦ πνεύματος,
ὅ ἐστιν ῥῆμα Θεοῦ,
¹⁸διὰ πάσης προσευχῆς καὶ δεήσεως, προσευχόμενοι
ἐν παντὶ καιρῷ ἐν Πνεύματι,
καὶ εἰς αὐτὸ ἀγρυπνοῦντες
ἐν πάσῃ προσκαρτερήσει.

Ephesians 6:10–18

¹⁰For the *coming time*
Make yourselves strong in the Kyrios
And in the force of his strength.
¹¹Put on the *full armour* of God
So that you can stand within yourself
Against the impact of the *Diabolos*
¹²For it is not given to us
To struggle against blood and flesh,
But against Archai,
Against Exousiai,
Against the great powers of this darkness,
Against the spirits of the evil under the heavens.
¹³Therefore take up the full armour of God
So that you might withstand the evil on its day
And as those who have overcome all,
May stand
¹⁴Be now steadfast
Gird your waist with *truth*
Clothe your *breast* with justice
¹⁵And shoe your feet with the readiness
For the gospel of peace.
¹⁶Above all, take up the shield of *faith*
With which you can quench all the arrows of evil,
All those made with fire
¹⁷And take the *helmet* of *the Saviour*
And the *sword* of the spirit:
That is the word of God.
¹⁸In all this, invoke in your petitions and prayers,
In every *instant* of the Spirit;
Be *vigilant*
In *persevering fidelity.*

'For it is not given to us to struggle against blood and flesh, but against Archai, against Exousiai, against the great powers of this darkness, against the spirits of the evil under the heavens' (verse 12). Evil, as a reality pertaining to all people, is addressed with great clarity in this verse. It does not appear as an abstraction, but rather as a spiritual cosmic power, with the same nomenclature as those to be found in the angelic hierarchies. To counter these 'great powers of this darkness', omnipresent in the world and latent within man, it is necessary to 'put on Christ' (Gal.3:27) as one would a suit of armour. Preceding passages have made it clear that this leads to *a stepping into* the light: 'For now you are light in the Lord. Live as children of light' (Eph.5:8).

The image of the armour of a Roman soldier may appear at first to be unpropitious. But if we succeed in overcoming the apparently martial connotations of the superficial image, then we discover a quiet inner picture indicating a streaming spiritual protective garment of light. This apparel is not simply grace-given, but must be *actively* acquired: the entire text is full of imperatives and challenges to those addressed – 'Make yourselves strong ... put on ... take up ... gird ... clothe ... invoke ... be vigilant,' and so forth.

Let us examine in more detail the diversity of the description. What is striking is the dynamic of the movement up and down when we follow the description of the parts of the body. This dynamic reflects the workings of divine beings which envelops and illuminates the entire human being, like raiment of light.

It commences with the protective attire as a whole (full armour, verse 11);
descends to the *waist* (truth, verse 14);
from there back up to the centre, the *breast* (justice, verse 14);
down to the *feet* (peace, verse 15);
then up to the *left hand* (the shield of faith, verse 16);
then further to the *head* (the helmet of the Saviour, of Christ, verse 17);
and down to the *right hand* (the sword of the spirit, the word of God, verse 17).

The image of the 'warrior of Light' culminates in three appeals:

— to grasp the moment, the *kairos,* in active prayer,
— to be vigilant in oneself, as a shepherd is with his sheep
— to live in fidelity to the spiritual world

In this picture of the ascending and descending forces in the human being – which through this dynamic has a certain sonorous character – the separate regions of the body are allotted particular spiritual values. Values such as *truth, justice, peace* and *belief* have to be striven for. We are not merely presented with a catalogue of precepts, and exhorted to adhere to the listed values.

Should we follow in our imagination the invitation to 'put on' these spiritual-moral values, like separate parts of a flowing, moving armour of light, we may begin to experience in ourselves and grasp with our thinking something of this concrete image.

Paul is precise in the correspondences to the regions of the body: before single parts of the body are addressed, there is the whole image of the armour of light, emphasised by the word πανοπλια *(panoplia),* which stresses the distinctive fullness of the armour.

From this 'steadfast' image in its entirety, our attention is directed to the waist, which should be girded with 'truth'. An image out of the Old Testament, the archetypal struggle of Jacob with the angel, may rise before us. There too, the human struggle for truth found its central point in the waist. Suffering a dislocation, Jacob is nevertheless blessed, and is given the new name Israel, which means 'warrior of God'.

In medieval medicine the zodiac sign of Libra (the scales) was apportioned to the *waist*. We may recall the image of St Michael and the scales testing the weight of truth. The meaning of the Greek word for truth, ἀληθεια *(alētheia),* is 'that which shows and reveals itself, which steps into the light.'

The centre of the human being, the *breast* or thorax, as the next region, is the location of the life-rhythm of our breathing. It must be 'clothed' with 'justice'. This indicates that the soul may accrue the steady rhythm of the breath when weighing up what is right. It thereby finds the right measure in encountering the world.

The *feet* which spread 'peace', evoke images of the winged shoes of the divine messenger Hermes, as well as the great peace marches of our time. To bring peace, we must begin to take steps towards the great goal.

With the *left hand,* with its 'shield of faith or belief', protection is afforded the left side, the heart side, of the human being. The word 'belief' is related to 'love' and also to 'leaves'. The close relationship of these words indicates that belief is something akin to the healthy process of plant growth. We can infer from this that an active participation by the human being is necessary for this shield to 'flourish'.

Alongside the 'shield of faith', we are shown the importance of the 'helmet of the Saviour' or the 'helmet of healing' for the head, and, for the right hand, 'the sword of the spirit, the Word of God' which must be grasped. At this point, the evil is not addressed in its hierarchical spiritual form, but is named as that which attacks the human being: 'the arrows of evil' (verse 16).

The 'helmet of salvation' points in the Greek to Christ. The word σωτηρ *(sōtēr)* means 'saviour' but also 'healer'. It is striking that it is the head and its thinking capacity that require especial protection. And how should we understand the quality of the 'fiery arrows'? Are they good or bad? Do they bear fire and light, or fire and temptation, or scorching destruction?

For these perennial questions, the 'sword of the spirit that is the word of God' may serve as a point of orientation. For μαχαιρα *(machaira),* the word for sword, signifies not merely the object, but also the power of discernment. Thus, the word of God is that which can discern. Within the dynamic interweaving of the three-in-one of the divine Trinity we find this power of discernment as 'word of God', the Logos, which manifests in the form of the Christ.[12]

The standard of the 'discerning power, which is the word of God' can be taken up by awakening human beings. As it is expressed in another passage in the Letter to the Ephesians (5:14):

> Awaken sleeper
> And arise from the dead
> And Christ shall be your light.

In this way our text concerning the awakening warrior, receiving grace *and* himself being active, can be an image for our current Michaelic time. For to stand against these 'great powers of darkness' who are omnipresent and at work in our inner and outer world, we must struggle anew every moment for the armour of light.

*Καὶ ὁ λόγος σὰρξ ἐγένετο
καὶ ἐσκήνωσεν ἐν ἡμῖν,
καὶ ἐθεασάμεθα τὴν δόξαν αὐτοῦ,
δόξαν ὡς μονογενοῦς παρὰ Πατρός,
πλήρης χάριτος καὶ ἀληθείας.*

Advent

In the beginning – the Logos

(John 1:1–18)

> And the Logos has become flesh
> And has erected his tent in us
> And we have seen his revelation-glory,
> A revelation as the once-born Son from the Father,
> Full of grace and truth.
> (John 1:14)

In contrast to the other three evangelists, John begins his gospel with a prologue, a unique mantric, hymnal text, which commences with rhythm and sonority like a powerful chant. From cosmic origins of the creation of the world to the existence of human life on earth – all are brought into the nexus of contemporary historical events, the appearance of John the Baptist as the prophet of Christ Jesus. One theme dominates the entire piece: the path of the Logos, from the creation of the world to the descent of the Logos-Christ into the earthly world and into a human body.

The sentence quoted above is the centrepiece and apex of the entire testimony, showing God taking on bodily form that allows human beings on earth to see the divine glory of revelation *(δόξα, doxa)*. With this sentence we pass as if through a gate into a story out of Exodus, the Second Book of Moses, which also concerns seeing God. There Moses asks God to be permitted just once to behold his revelation-glory (כבד *kevod)*. Moses, the spiritual leader and mediator between God and his people Israel,

וַיֹּאמַר הַרְאֵנִי נָא אֶת־כְּבֹדֶךָ ¹⁸
וַיֹּאמֶר אֲנִי אַעֲבִיר כָּל־טוּבִי עַל־פָּנֶיךָ ¹⁹
וְקָרָאתִי בְשֵׁם יְהוָה לְפָנֶיךָ וְחַנֹּתִי אֶת־אֲשֶׁר
אָחֹן וְרִחַמְתִּי אֶת־אֲשֶׁר אֲרַחֵם:
²⁰וַיֹּאמֶר לֹא תוּכַל לִרְאֹת אֶת־פָּנָי כִּי לֹא־
יִרְאַנִי הָאָדָם וָחָי:
²¹וַיֹּאמֶר יְהוָה הִנֵּה מָקוֹם אִתִּי וְנִצַּבְתָּ
עַל־הַצּוּר: ²²וְהָיָה בַּעֲבֹר כְּבֹדִי וְשַׂמְתִּיךָ
בְּנִקְרַת הַצּוּר וְשַׂכֹּתִי כַפִּי עָלֶיךָ עַד־עָבְרִי:
²³וַהֲסִרֹתִי אֶת־כַּפִּי וְרָאִיתָ אֶת־אֲחֹרָי וּפָנַי
לֹא יֵרָאוּ

is granted his wish. However, he needs the necessary protection: covered by the hand of God and placed by him in a cleft in the rock as the revelation-glory passes, Moses only beholds the beauty, sound and the after-effects of the divine.

> [18] And Moses spoke, 'Let me indeed behold your majesty!'
> [19] And [Yahweh] spoke, 'I will let all my beauty pass before your face, and I will proclaim my name, YAHWEH, before your face. All my grace to whom I will be gracious, and all my mercy to whom I will be merciful.'
> [20] And he spoke, 'You may not look upon my face; for no man may behold me and live.'
> [21] And Yahweh spoke, 'See, there is a place near me where you shall stand upon the rock. [22] And it will happen thus: as my glory passes by, I shall place you in the cleft of the rock, and with my hand I shall shield you from my passing by. [23] When I remove my hand, you shall see my back; but my face may not be seen.' (Exod.33:18–23).

May we infer from this that the true beholding of God face to face in all the divine glory was not possible for man before the time of the incarnation of the Logos-Christ? As is indicated in the above passage, and as an old saying intimates: 'He who sees God, dies.'

As if in answer to this, in the Prologue of John's Gospel we hear the mighty announcement, 'We have looked upon his Revelation-Glory.'

This can first be spoken by John *after* the life, death and resurrection of Christ. God becomes visible through Christ, and as Father may be called upon. 'Whoever beholds me, beholds the Father' (John 14:9), and 'Nobody comes to the Father except through me' (John 14:6), as Christ expresses it.

But what may we understand by 'beholding God'? We shall return to this question. First, however, let us look at the entire text of the Prologue in this attempt to translate the enigmatic original.

Ἐν ἀρχῇ ἦν ὁ Λόγος,
καὶ ὁ Λόγος ἦν πρὸς τὸν Θεόν,
καὶ Θεὸς ἦν ὁ Λόγος·
²οὗτος ἦν ἐν ἀρχῇ πρὸς τὸν Θεόν·
³πάντα δι' αὐτοῦ ἐγένετο,
καὶ χωρὶς αὐτοῦ ἐγένετο οὐδὲ ἕν
ὃ γέγονεν ⁴ἐν αὐτῷ ζωὴ ἦν,
καὶ ἡ ζωὴ ἦν τὸ φῶς τῶν ἀνθρώπων·
⁵καὶ τὸ φῶς ἐν τῇ σκοτίᾳ φαίνει,
καὶ ἡ σκοτία αὐτὸ οὐ κατέλαβεν.
⁶Ἐγένετο ἄνθρωπος,
ἀπεσταλμένος παρὰ Θεοῦ,
ὄνομα αὐτῷ Ἰωάννης·
⁷οὗτος ἦλθεν εἰς μαρτυρίαν,
ἵνα μαρτυρήσῃ περὶ τοῦ φωτός,
ἵνα πάντες πιστεύσωσιν δι' αὐτοῦ·
⁸οὐκ ἦν ἐκεῖνος τὸ φῶς,
ἀλλ' ἵνα μαρτυρήσῃ περὶ τοῦ φωτός.
⁹Ἦν τὸ φῶς τὸ ἀληθινόν,
ὃ φωτίζει πάντα ἄνθρωπον,
ἐρχόμενον εἰς τὸν κόσμον·
¹⁰ἐν τῷ κόσμῳ ἦν,
καὶ ὁ κόσμος δι' αὐτοῦ ἐγένετο,
καὶ ὁ κόσμος αὐτὸν οὐκ ἔγνω·
¹¹εἰς τὰ ἴδια ἦλθεν,
καὶ οἱ ἴδιοι αὐτὸν οὐ παρέλαβον·
¹²ὅσοι δὲ ἔλαβον αὐτόν,
ἔδωκεν αὐτοῖς ἐξουσίαν
τέκνα Θεοῦ γενέσθαι,
τοῖς πιστεύουσιν εἰς τὸ ὄνομα αὐτοῦ,
¹³οἳ οὐκ ἐξ αἱμάτων
οὐδὲ ἐκ θελήματος σαρκὸς
οὐδὲ ἐκ θελήματος ἀνδρὸς
ἀλλ' ἐκ Θεοῦ ἐγεννήθησαν.

¹In the *inner space* of the primal forces *was and is*
  working the Logos,
And the Logos is *in movement* toward the God
And a divine being is the Logos.
²He was *in movement* toward the God.
³Through him, everything entered into existence
And without him, nothing entered into existence.
⁴*What existed*, was in him and is life
And the life is the light of men,
⁵And the light shines within the darkness
And the darkness has not *overcome it.*
⁶A man became,
And was sent out by the divine world,
Given to him was the name John.
⁷He came as a witness
That he give testimony of the light,
That all may *believe* through him.
⁸He was not the light,
But rather would he give testimony of the light.
⁹The light, the revealed,
That enlightens every man
Was and is come into the world.
¹⁰He is in the world
And the world was made through him,
And the world has not recognised him.
¹¹Unto his own he *came and comes*
And his own did not accept him.
¹²Those, however, who accepted him,
To those he gives power
To be born out of God –
Those who in raising, unfold themselves, into his name,
¹³Not out of the blood
Nor of the will of the body,
And not out of the will of man,
But are born out of God.

¹⁴Καὶ ὁ Λόγος σὰρξ ἐγένετο
καὶ ἐσκήνωσεν ἐν ἡμῖν,
καὶ ἐθεασάμεθα τὴν δόξαν αὐτοῦ,
δόξαν ὡς μονογενοῦς παρὰ Πατρός,
πλήρης χάριτος καὶ ἀληθείας.
¹⁵Ἰωάννης μαρτυρεῖ περὶ αὐτοῦ καὶ κέκραγεν λέγων·
Οὗτος ἦν ὃν εἶπον·
Ὁ ὀπίσω μου ἐρχόμενος ἔμπροσθέν μου γέγονεν,
ὅτι πρῶτός μου ἦν·
¹⁶ὅτι ἐκ τοῦ πληρώματος αὐτοῦ ἡμεῖς πάντες ἐλάβομεν,
καὶ χάριν ἀντὶ χάριτος·
¹⁷ὅτι ὁ νόμος διὰ Μωϋσέως ἐδόθη,
ἡ χάρις καὶ ἡ ἀλήθεια
διὰ Ἰησοῦ Χριστοῦ ἐγένετο.
¹⁸Θεὸν οὐδεὶς ἑώρακεν πώποτε:
μονογενὴς Θεὸς
ὁ ὢν εἰς τὸν κόλπον τοῦ Πατρὸς,
ἐκεῖνος ἐξηγήσατο.

> [14] And the Logos has become flesh
> And *has erected his tent in* us
> *And we have seen his revelation-glory,*
> A revelation as the once-born Son from the Father,
> Full of grace and truth.
> [15] John testifies of him and has called out:
> This is he from whom I said
> That he, coming after me, was before me,
> Because he precedes me,
> [16] From his *fullness*, we have all received
> Grace upon grace.
> [17] Because the law was given through Moses,
> Grace and truth
> Entered into existence through Jesus Christ.
> [18] Nobody has ever seen God.
> The once-born Son,
> Who living in the being of the Father,
> He it is, who leads to him.

The prologue begins vigorously and recalls almost verbatim the beginning of Genesis. With the first two words, ἐν ἀρχῃ *(en archē),* we have a presentiment of the 'inner space' of a cosmic commencement or *initi*ation. Perhaps, we can picture both time and space as initiated. The preposition ἐν 'in, within' is spatial, while containing temporal connotations, such as 'in the beginning'. I have attempted to reflect this in the formulation 'In the *inner-space* of the primal forces ...'

Following directly is ἦν *(ēn),* the imperfect, usually translated as *'was'.* Yet this verb form is not simply a grammatical indication of the past, but primarily indicates an *unfinished deed.* Thus with this verb form, the text tells us that the Logos *'was* and *is'* effective and alive even until now, the moment of speaking it.

In the same verse, we read that 'the Logos *was* and *is (ἦν) in movement towards* God'. The preposition πρός *(pros)* with the accusative can mean 'towards ... to' and indicates a movement with a direction. We may carefully ask if, in this hymn to the creation which names the Christ-Logos and the Father-God, the small but significant *pros* is an allusion to the Holy Spirit, active in all movement of creation? If so, then the divinity would be addressed in its comprehensive form: the Trinity as a *process*, as a living movement, as a harmony.

The Logos-Christ is not described here as being *with* the Father God, and thereby inert (as in the Vulgate translation *apud Deum*). Rather, the Logos appears as the aspect of Christ in creating, in the *process* of the three-in-one of the Trinity.

This being alive in creating is particularly emphasised again in verse 4, where the small relative clause 'what existed' is not attached onto verse 3 but, as we can clearly see in the earliest manuscripts, begins the next sentence, 'What existed was in him, and is life.'[1]

Augustine, who also began the sentence anew with 'what existed', explained the relationship between this aliveness in the idea and the finished created thing in the following way:

> The carpenter makes a chest. First, he has the chest as a creative idea, for if he did not have it as a creative idea, how could he produce it? ... The *finished* chest is not life, the chest as *idea* is life, because the soul of its creator lives. The soul is where the ideas are before they manifest. ... Because the wisdom of God through which everything exists, contains all ideas before creating them, that which is to be created by the idea is therefore not immediately itself already life, *but everything which has been created, is life in God.*[2]

Also the trusted passage in verse 5, often translated as, 'and the light shone in the darkness, but the darkness has not understood it,' gains a quite different content if we examine the verb in all its variety of meaning. *Katelaben* (from καταλαμβανω) can be 'to grasp, understand', but its underlying meaning concerns a struggle: 'to capture, occupy, raid, attack, hit, hold, overwhelm, oppress, force, to be hostile.'³ So I have translated: 'And the light shines within the darkness *and* the darkness has not *overcome* it.' Here και *(kai)* simply means 'and', and not 'but'.

So light and darkness are two forces weaving within each other, and the darkness 'cannot overcome' the light. Light is the decisive factor; it is stronger, but both are there – just as the adversary powers are always there, as indeed they must be.

The verb πιστευω *(pisteuō)* 'to believe', in verses 7 and 12 takes on a new resonance if we consider its roots. As we saw in the previous chapter, the word 'belief' is related to 'love' and also to 'leaves'. The close relationship of these words can bring up the image of a tree coming into leaf, and this gives the word a fresh, living and growing meaning.

In verse 9, there are two possibilities for the translation. First: '[The Logos] was and is the true light which enlightens every man coming into the world,' or, secondly: '[the Logos] was and is the true light coming into the world, and which enlightens ...'

Thus everyone who comes into the world is enlightened by the true Logos-light, and the Logos is the true light that has come into the world. Both translations are grammatically possible and correct. We should try to hear both simultaneously.

In verse 11 the verb is in the aorist form, which as I have often pointed out is the boundless tense. In order to draw attention to this, I have expressed it in two tenses, 'Unto his own he *came and comes.*'

If we speak the Prologue aloud in its entirety, whether in Greek or our own language (regardless of translation), we can sense how the rhythm carries us relentlessly forward through its breath and its sounds, and beyond that there is the profound universality of its content. In verse 14 it reaches the climax when its sounds and rhythms come to rest as if having 'arrived', in the words 'And the Logos has become flesh and *has erected his tent in* us.'

In a few lofty words the incarnation of God is touched on here in the first part of the sentence, but nonetheless it remains a mystery. In the second part of the sentence, the word 'tent' σκηνη *(skēnē)* appears. This word is used to indicate the place where the divine will manifest itself in the world, and is a motif that spans the whole Bible. From the holy tent, the tabernacle of the Old Testament, also known as the 'tent of revelation' through to the 'great voice' of the Apocalypse, which cries, 'behold the tent of God among men'.[4] This repeatedly used word is variously translated as tent or tabernacle but sometimes as dwelling, booth or hut; this obscures the otherwise transparent clarity of the same word. In what sense is the word 'tent' used in the Old and New Testaments?

During the wandering through the desert of the people of Israel, the sacred tent was the centre of their lives. In this 'tent of revelation', the most sacrosanct which only the High Priest could enter once a year, the Ark of the Covenant was kept. On its lid was embossed the image of two cherubim. In the empty space above their entwining wings, hidden in the dark, God appeared to the initiates.

In the New Testament, this place of appearance of the divine is termed the 'tent' nineteen times.[5] The most obvious example is the reference by the synoptic writers at the Transfiguration. The word used in all three gospels is 'tent' – usually translated as 'tabernacle' or 'tent'. Three chosen disciples, Peter, John and James, are 'taken up' by Christ, and experience a lofty and overwhelming vision of the divine: the Transfiguration of Christ. Peter wishes to hold on to this moment, and asks if he may build 'three tents' for this divine manifestation.

In the Prologue of John's Gospel, the 'tent' can be seen as a mighty metamorphosis of the dwelling of the divine in the Old and New Testament, when it speaks of the incarnating Christ-Logos as having 'erected his tent in us.' From this new inwardness which echoes the beginning of the Prologue ('in the inner space of the primal forces'), the beholding of God acquires a completely new dimension. In this part of the Prologue, a double-activity is referred to. The divine world has 'erected its tent' in man. That is the 'fullness' referred to in verse 16, which can receive 'grace upon grace'. But in order to behold God, the inner activity of the individual, his grace-given spiritual attentiveness is necessary. In a *kairos,* that is, in a special moment of one's life, the 'beholding of God' can be present as an event of illumination. Under the impact of such a re-cognition – whether in nature, art or in a real encounter with another, we can experience an 'I am you'.

Through contemplating such words and their connotations, the lofty spirit of the Prologue of the Gospel of John can lead us to such a beholding. That is Advent as a perpetual possibility.

Notes

The original Greek texts follow Nestle & Aland, *Novum Testamentum Graece*, occasionally using variants from the Apparatus. The original Hebrew texts follow Kittel, *Biblia Hebraica*.

Introduction

1 Origen states that Holy Scripture has body, soul and spirit. The literal or historical meaning is its body, the moral is its soul, and the allegorical or spiritual meaning is its spirit. Simpler people should be edified by the obvious meaning, the straightforward historical sense. The more educated should find edification for their souls by the moral meaning. The perfect should be edified by the mystical or spiritual sense with relation to Christ, or the spiritual law, as it contains the shadow of the blessings to come. *(On First Principles,* Book 4).

2 Hellenised second names were common at the time of the Jewish Diaspora. Saul did not change his name because of his conversion and baptism, but used both names since birth. Luke mentions both names as valid (Acts 13:9). See also the description of the Letter to the Ephesians in the Michaelmas chapter.

3 The legend is first told in the pseudepigraphic Letter of Aristeas, a Hellenistic Jew living at the time of Ptolemy II. Both Josephus and Philo cite him. According to the legend, 72 Jewish scholars were entrusted with the translation, 6 from each of the 12 tribes of Israel.

4 I am indebted for this indication to an unpublished lecture manuscript by Karl Friedrich Althoff, January 1979.

5 The word *agapē* is used with this particular meaning of love in various passages, for instance John 5:42; 13:35; 15:10, 13; 17:26 and as a verb in 21:15. See 'Agape, divine love in the Fourth Gospel' in Frieling, *New Testament Studies,* where a wealth of examples and passages are examined.

6 Steiner, *Das Geheimnis der Trinität,* lecture of July 23, 1922, p. 24.

7 The first three *(Trivium* in Latin) were known as the 'arts of the logos' or language; the following four *(Quadrivium)* as the 'arts of the number'. The four arts of the number (arithmetic, geometry, astronomy and music) were already named by Plato alongside philosophy in his *Politeia* as integral for the education of every statesperson. Plato borrowed from the mystery wisdom of the Pythagoreans. See Burkert, *Lore and Science in Ancient Pythagoreanism.*

8 See Cardaun, *Marcus Terentius Varro*.
9 Zekl, *Marianus Capella*.
10 Teichmann, *Der Mensch und sein Tempel: Chartres*, p. 107.
11 Wittkower, *Allegory and the Migration of Symbols*.

Advent

1 For instance in the Sermon on the Mount (Matt.5) and in Teaching in the Synagogue (Luke 4:16–30).
2 Many references to this in Gesenius, *Hebräisches und aramäisches Handwörterbuch*.
3 Examples are in Körner *Hebräisches Studiengrammatik*, p. 316.
4 Compare the beatitudes of the Sermon on the Mount. There too, the first sentence refers to those who 'hunger for the spirit' (Matt.5:3).

Christmas

1 Steiner, listener's notes of a lecture of Dec 30, 1904, in *Beiträge zur Rudolf Steiner Gesamtausgabe*, No. 60, 1977.
2 See Strack & Billerbeck, *Kommentar zum Neuen Testament*, and Lauenstein, *Der Messias*, pp. 27–106.
3 For a wider understanding of the term *doxa*, see the thirteenth-century mystic Mechthild of Magdeburg, who describes her visions of God in *The Flowing Light of the Godhead*.
4 The Essenes were a strict and ascetic Jewish community of believers who awaited the end of times and the appearance of the two messianic figures in their own time. Among the authors of antiquity who wrote about them were Pliny the Elder in *Naturalis Historia* (5:73), Philo of Alexandria in *Quod Omnis Probus Liber*, (72.91); Josephus in *De Bello Judaico* (2:119–161).
5 Kurt Schubert in *Zeitschrift für Kath. Theol.* 74/1952, p.53. Also Medico, *Deux Manuscripts hebreux*, p.33 and M. Black 'Servants of the Lord and Son of Man' *Scottish Journal of Theology*, 6, 1953, pp.1–11.
6 Schubert in *Judaica*, 11, 1955. The 18 references translated and commented upon in my book *Zepter und Stern*. The literature on this research has been recorded by J.A. Fitzmyer, 'The Aramaic Elect of God: Text from Qumran Cave 4' in *Catholic Biblical Quarterly*, 27, 1965, pp. 348–72.
7 See Woude, *Die messianischen Vorstellungen der Gemeinde von Qumran*.
8 Steiner, *According to Luke*, and *The Spiritual Guidance*.

Between Epiphany and Passiontide

1 In Genesis 33:18–20 Shechem is named as the place where Jacob bought land and built an altar. Later Joshua brought all twelve tribes of Israel together in Shechem after the conquering and settlement of the whole of Canaan (13th century BC), and made them swear an oath of allegiance to

NOTES

the one God Yahweh, who had called their fathers and released them from Egypt.
2 There were two major deportations of the people of Israel: the Assyrian exile in 721 BC and the Babylonian in 587–538 BC. The five peoples who were settled in Samaria were from Babylon, Cuthah, Avva, Hamath and Sepharvaim (2Kings 17:24–31).
3 Zerubbabbel came from royal lineage, a descendant of David, and appears also in the genealogy of Jesus as one of his forefathers (Matt.1:12).
4 There are also non-biblical references to the enmity between Jews and Samaritans, for instance, Josephus in A*ntiquitates Judaicae* (11:8,2) writes that the Temple at Gerizim was destroyed by Jews in the year 128 BC.
5 The five husbands have been equated with the five foreign gods who were forced upon Samaria when foreign settlers came. See Barrett, *The Gospel according to St. John.*
6 Schnackenburg, *Das Johannesevangelium,* Vol. 1, p. 467.
7 For instance in Sifre to Deuteronomy 11:22 §48 (84a) quoted by Strack & Billerbeck, *Kommentar zum Neuen Testament,* Vol. 2, p. 435 (and further extensive reference pp. 433–36). I owe this reference to an essay by Friedhelm Wessel, 'Die Beziehung zwischen Jesus und der Torah nach Joh. 4:16–19.' in *Biblische Notizen,* No.68, 1993, pp. 26–34.
8 Origen, *Commentary on John,* Book 13, fragment 18.
9 Self-revelation as the 'I-am' is also found in John's Gospel in 6:20; 8:24, 28, 58; 13:19; 18:5, 8.
10 Exod.3:14: 'I will be, who I will be'; Deut.32:39: 'I, I am'.
11 Rev.22:17: 'And the spirit and the bride speak: Come! And those who hear this shall also speak: Come! And those who thirst shall come; and those who desire it, shall take the water of life freely.'
12 Steiner, *The Gospel of John*, lecture of May 23, 1908.

Passiontide

1 Amongst others Isaiah 7:14, the prophecy of the immanent Immanuel. Also Isa.42:1–4; 49:1–6; 50:4–9; 52:13–53:12.
2 By comparison, survivors of concentration camps used biblical texts to help them describe and understand their own experiences, which were often beyond words. See Wiesel, *Noah's warning.*
3 Steiner, *According to Matthew,* lecture of Sep 12, 1910.
4 Hence the title of his book, *Christianity as Mystical Fact.* The mystery character of early Christianity is now also accepted by mainstream research which references Steiner, for instance, Kloft, *Mysterienkulte der Antike,* p. 110.

Easter Sunday

1 Matt.27:55, 61; Mark 15:47; 16:1–5, 9; Luke 7:36–50; 8:2 John 12:1–8; 20:11–18. The Gospels of Philip, Thomas, Mary Magdalene, Pistis Sophia and the Legenda Aurea of Jacobus de Voragine.
2 From the whole range of novels on the subject, the best known is perhaps Dan Brown's thriller, *The Da Vinci Code,* with its wildly invented 'facts'.
3 See Schiller, *Iconography of Christian Art.*
4 The verb στρεφω *(strephō)* can mean to turn towards, to face (Matt.5:39); to devote (Acts 13:46); to turn around (Matt.7:6); to bring back (Matt.27:3); to convert (Matt.18:3, John 12:40) and to change (Rev.11:6).
5 The two disciples on the way to Emmaus also take the Risen One to be someone fitting into the surroundings, merely another wayfarer (Luke 24:15).
6 Participle, aorist passive, feminine nominative singular.
7 *Behold:* εωρακας, οραω *(heōrakas, horaō)* to look up, to behold (John 19:37); perceive, notice (Matt.28:7); to experience, to go through (Luke 17:22). *Seeing:* ιδοντες, ιδειν *(idontes, idein)* to see, catch sight of, a sense experienced through the eye (Matt.2:2); to be conscious of (Matt.27:54); to look on something, regard (1John 3:1; Acts 15:6); to see something, to take a look at (1Pet.3:10).
8 Μακαριος *(makarios)* mostly translated as 'blessed', does not imply a passive state of bliss, but rather 'large, wide, secure in itself, resting in itself'.
9 Steiner, *From Limestone to Lucifer,* lecture of May 9, 1923, p. 224.
10 Steiner, *From Jesus to Christ,* lecture of Oct 5, 1911, pp. 19f.

Eastertime

1 Experiences of the Risen Christ in a group are to be found at Ascension (Acts 1:4ff), Whitsun (Acts 2:1ff), and when the disciples were together in one accord (John 20:19ff; 21:1ff). An exception is the encounter of Mary Magdalene who is alone when Christ appears, as we saw in the previous chapter.
2 In English we would clearly use 'opened-up' as the revealing gesture, but the author wishes to draw our attention to the subtle difference that unfolds when we use 'through' (the clearest connotation of the Greek *dia)* as the prefix *(Translator).*
3 Frieling, *Christologische Aufsätze,* p. 156. See also *New Testament Studies,* p. 104.

Ascension

1 The sixth century Christian author of *Celestial Hierarchy* used the name Dionysus the Areopagite from the Acts of the Apostles (17:34). He is also known as Pseudo-Dionysus. The hierarchy of the Exousiai are called Spirits of Form by Steiner *(Foundations of Esotericism,* lecture of Oct 8, 1905).
2 Steiner, *Approaching the Mystery of Golgotha,* lecture of Oct 14, 1913, p. 7.

NOTES

Whitsun

1 The second reference is in Paul's sermon to the Athenians as he speaks to them in the agora of the 'unknown God', who has given all people ζωη *(zōē)* life, and πνοη *(pnoē)* spirit (Acts 17:25).
2 The wisdom literature of the Old Testament includes the Book of Job, the Book of Proverbs, Ecclesiastes (or the Preacher), the Song of Songs, the Book of Wisdom (or Wisdom of Solomon), Sirach (or Ecclesiasticus) and the Book of Baruch.
3 Sir.1:1–9, 24:1–18 & 23–29; Prov. 3:13–26, 4:1–9 & 20–23, 8:1 & 12–21, 9:1–6, 31:10–31; Wisdom 1:6–15, 6:12–16, 7:4–21, 8:3–21, 9:1–19, 10:9–19, 11:1–5; Baruch 3:9–14 & 29–38, 4:1–4. See Schipflinger, *Sophia-Maria.*
4 The seldom used word אמון *(amun)* which otherwise appears only in Jeremiah (52:15) means foreman, work-master. The Vulgate translates this correspondingly as *conponens,* which can be rendered as co-perpetrator. The Septuagint translates this passage with άρμαζουσα *(harmazousa),*'joiner together'. In English versions, the King James has simply 'brought up', more modern versions have 'master craftsman', 'master workman' or 'architect'.

St John's Tide

1 The Hebrew root of הנורא *(hanora)* means 'to shine' and has the double connotation of 'fear' and 'awe' in relation to the divine.
2 Matt.3, Mark 1:4–14, Luke 1:5–17, 1:39–80, 3:1–22, John 1:6–8, 1:19–35; Q source 3:7.9; Koran in the Maryam Sura (19:7, 19:12–15); Josephus, *Antiquities,* 18:5.2 (see also Mason, *Josephus and the New Testament*).
3 See Ernst, *Johannes der Täufer,* p. 288 footnote 75.
4 Codex Sinaiticus, Codex Vaticanus, both of which belong to the oldest extant handwritten biblical scripts (around AD 350). The first written form of the Gospel of Mark is generally agreed to be about AD 70.
5 John 6:35, 48, 51; 8:12; 10:7, 9, 11, 14; 11:25; 14:6 & 15:1, 5.
6 Steiner, *The Principle of Spiritual Economy,* lecture of April 10, 1909.

Michaelmas

1 Chorin, *Paulus,* p. 12.
2 Gamaliel later defended his erstwhile pupil Paul and helped him and several other apostles avoid the punishment of being stoned in Jerusalem (Acts 5:34–42).
3 Was the experience a conversion, vocation or an initiation? Paul's Damascus experience is subject to differences of opinion and interpretation in theological circles to this day. Strecker, in *Die liminale Theologie des Paulus,* holds the view that the Damascus experience was an initiation. Steiner put forward this view already in 1910 in his lectures *Genesis: Secrets of Creation.*
4 Acts 9:1–22; 22:6–16; 26:12; Gal.1:15; Phil.3:7; 1Cor.15:8; 2Cor.4:1–5.

5 Haase & Temporini, *Aufstieg und Niedergang,* Vol. 3; Hengel, *Judentum und Hellenismus.*
6 Steiner, *The Principle of Spiritual Economy,* lecture of March 31, 1909.
7 It could well have been that the apostles simply would not have acknowledged the erstwhile persecutor.
8 Rom.6:3, 8:17; Eph.2:6; Col.2:12; 3:1.
9 For a detailed portrayal of the clearly substantiated research results see Biser, *Paulus,* p. 26. On Ephesians, see Sellin, *Der Brief an die Epheser,* and Pokorny, *Der Brief des Paulus an die Epheser.*
10 Biser, *Paulus,* p. 27.
11 See Welburn, *The Beginnings of Christianity,* and Kriby, *Ephesians, Baptism and Pentecost.*
12 The original text here (Eph.6:17) is ῥῆμα Θεου, *rhema Theou.* The word *rhema* (word) and *logos* (word) are etymologically related and are often used interchangeably in the New Testament.

Advent

1 John Scotus Erigena also begins verse 4 with 'What has become', See Klünker, *Denken im Gespräch mit dem Engel,* p. 77. Corresponding punctuation is found in Nestle & Aland, *Novum Testamentum Graece.*
2 Augustine, *Tractatus in Iohannis Euangelium* 35:1 in Augustinus, *Ausgewählten Schriften,* Vol.5.
3 This bellicose sense appears in 1Cor. 9:24 and John 12:35.
4 The holy tent אהל *'ohel* in Hebrew, (*Tabernacalum* in Latin) is described in Exod.25 and 36. Also Exod.27:21 and Rev.21:3.
5 Matt.17:4, Mark 9:5, Luke 9:33, 16:9, Acts 7:43 & 44, 15:16, Heb.8:2, 9:2,3,6,8, 11, 11:9, 13:10, Rev.13:6, 15:5, 21:3.

Bibliography

Augustinus, Aurelius, *Ausgewählten Schriften,* tr. Johannes Specht, Kempten 1913.
Barrett, C.K. *The Gospel According to St John,* SPCK 2009.
Biser, Eugen, *Paulus: Zeuge, Mystiker, Vordenker,* Munich 1992.
Burkert, Walter, *Lore and Science in Ancient Pythagoreanism,* Harvard 1974.
Cardaun, Burckhardt, *Marcus Terentius Varro,* Heidelberg 2001.
Chorin, Schalom Ben, *Paulus: Der Völkerapostel in jüdischer Sicht,* München 1980.
Debus, Michael, *Mary and Sophia: the Feminine Element in the Spiritual Evolution of Humanity,* Floris Books 2013.
Ernst, Joseph, *Johannes der Täufer,* (supplement to *Zeitschrift für die Neutestamentliche Wissenschaft und die Kunde der Älteren Kirche,* Vol. 53) Berlin 1989.
Frieling, Rudolf, *Christologische Aufsätze,* Stuttgart 1982.
Frieling, Rudolf, *New Testament Studies,* Floris 1994.
Gesenius, W. *Hebräisches und aramäisches Handwörterbuch,* Berlin 1962.
Goethe, *Italian Journey,* Penguin 1985.
Haase, Wolfgang & Temporini, Hildegard, *Aufstieg und Niedergang der Römischen Welt,* Göttingen 1979.
Hengel, Martin, *Judentum und Hellenismus,* Tübingen 1966.
Kittel, Rudolf, *Biblia Hebraica,* Stuttgart 1990.
Kloft, Hans, *Mysterienkulte der Antike,* München 2006.
Klünker, Wolf Ulrich, *Denken im Gespräch mit dem Engel,* Stuttgart 1988.
Körner, Jutta, *Hebräisches Studiengrammatik,* Leipzig 1998.
Kriby, J.C. *Ephesians, Baptism and Pentecost,* London 1966.
Lauenstein, Dieter, *Der Messias,* Stuttgart 1971.
Mason, Steve, *Josephus and the New Testament,* Hendrickson 2003.
Mechthild of Magdeburg, *The Flowing Light of the Godhead,* tr. Frank Tobin, Paulist Press, New York 1998.
Medico, H.E. Del, *Deux Manuscripts hebreux de la Mer Morte,* Rais, 1951.
Nestle, Eberhard & Aland, Kurt, *Novum Testamentum Graece,* 27th ed, Stuttgart 2001.
Pokorny, Petr, *Der Brief des Paulus an die Epheser,* Berlin 1992.
Schiller, Gertrud, *Iconography of Christian Art,* Lund Humphries 1971.
Schipflinger, Thomas, *Sophia-Maria: Eine ganzheitliche Vision der Schöpfung,* München 1988.

Schnackenburg, Rudolf *Das Johannesevangelium*, Herder, Freiburg 1979.
Sellin, Gerhard, *Der Brief an die Epheser,* Göttingen 2008.
Steiner, Rudolf. Volume Nos refer to the Collected Works (CW), or to the German Gesamtausgabe (GA).
—, *According to Luke* (CW 114) SteinerBooks, USA 2001.
—, *According to Matthew* (CW 123) SteinerBooks, USA 2002.
—, *Approaching the Mystery of Golgotha* (CW 152) SteinerBooks, USA 2006.
—, *Christianity as Mystical Fact* (CW 8) Anthroposophic Press, USA 1997.
—, *Foundations of Esotericism* (CW 93a) Rudolf Steiner Press, UK 1983.
—, *From Jesus to Christ* (CW 131) Rudolf Steiner Press, UK 2005.
—, *From Limestone to Lucifer* (CW 349) Rudolf Steiner Press, UK 2000.
—, *Das Geheimnis der Trinität* (GA 214) Dornach 1999.
—, *Genesis: Secrets of Creation* (CW 122) Rudolf Steiner Press, UK 2003.
—, *The Gospel of John* (CW 103) Anthropsophic Press, USA 1984.
—, *The Principle of Spiritual Economy,* (CW 109) Anthroposophic Press, USA 1986.
—, *The Spiritual Guidance of the Individual and Humanity* (CW 15) Anthroposophic Press, USA 1992.
Strack, H.L. & Billerbeck, P. *Kommentar zum Neuen Testament aus Talmud und Midrasch,* München 1922–61.
Strecker, Christian, *Die liminale Theologie des Paulus,* Göttingen 1999.
Teichmann, Frank, *Der Mensch und sein Tempel: Chartres,* Urachhaus, Stuttgart 1991.
Welburn, Andrew, *The Beginnings of Christianity,* Floris Books 1991.
Weymann, Elsbeth, *Zepter und Stern: Die Erwartung von zwei Messiasgestalten in den Schriftsrollen von Qumran,* Stuttgart 1993.
Wiesel, Elie, *Noah's Warning,* University of Notre Dame, Indiana 1984.
Wittkower, Rudolf, *Allegory and the Migration of Symbols,* Thames & Hudson, London 1987.
Woude, A.S. van der, *Die messianischen Vorstellungen der Gemeinde von Qumran,* Assen 1957.
Zekl, Hans Günter, *Marianus Capella: Die Hochzeit der Philologia mit Merkur, De nuptiis Philologiae et Mercurii,* Würzburg 2005.

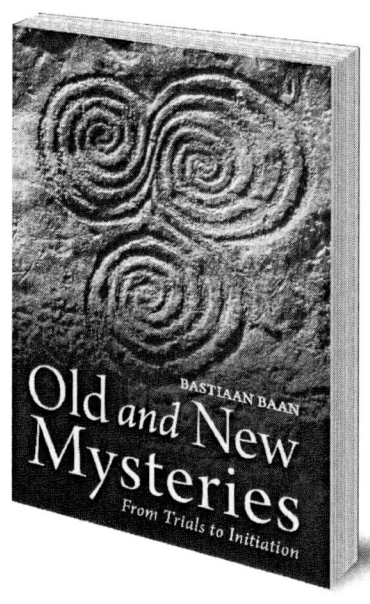

Old and New Mysteries

From Trials to Initiation

Bastiaan Baan

'Rich in references, rich in illustrations,
rich in knowledge and practical advice.'
– *New View*

There is great contemporary interest in the mystery centres of antiquity, such as prehistoric caves, the pyramids of Egypt, Newgrange in Ireland, and the Externsteine in Germany. The trials and rites that took place there were for the chosen few, and are vividly described in this book – from the trials of fire and water to the three-day near-death sleep.

The author goes on to argue that modern-day initiation, however, has a substantially different character. Whereas a 'hierophant' – a guide – was previously needed to navigate a trial, these days it is life itself which brings us trials, which can sometimes lead to deeper experiences of the spiritual.

www.florisbooks.co.uk

The Lord's Prayer and Rudolf Steiner

A study of his insights into the archetypal prayer of Christianity

Peter Selg

'Your will be done, on earth as it is in heaven.'

Rudolf Steiner once called the Lord's Prayer the 'greatest initiation prayer', and he spoke about it many times, also referring to it as the central prayer of Christian experience.

This book is, however, the first time that all of Steiner's comments, accounts and perspectives have been brought together in one place, presenting the full scope and depth of his ideas. Along the way, Peter Selg reveals some surprising insights into the spiritual history and mission of Christianity.

www.florisbooks.co.uk

Lord of the Elements

Interweaving Christianity and Nature

Bastiaan Baan

The four classical elements of earth, water, air and fire are present in Genesis and continue to be significant throughout Christianity. Different streams of thought, such as the School of Chartres, and Celtic Christianity, have emphasised the elements in different ways.

In this unique book, Bastiaan Baan, an experienced spiritual thinker, brings these elements together with ideas from Rudolf Steiner's anthroposophy. He considers, in particular, how elemental beings – nature spirits – relate to the four elements, and explores the role of elemental beings in our world.

This is a fascinating and original work on the connections between Christianity and the natural world.

www.florisbooks.co.uk

You may also be interested in
these books by Rudolf Frieling

Christianity and Islam

Christianity and Reincarnation

The Essence of Christianity

The Eucharist

Hidden Treasure in the Psalms

New Testament Studies

Old Testament Studies

www.florisbooks.co.uk